Effective

Youth

Ministry

Effective *Youth* Ministry

A Congregational Approach

ROLAND D. MARTINSON

AUGSBURG Publishing House • Minneapolis

EFFECTIVE YOUTH MINISTRY
A Congregational Approach

Copyright © 1988 Augsburg Publishing House

Scripture quotations unless otherwise noted are from the Holy Bible: New International Version. Copyright 1978 by the New York International Bible Society. Used by permission of Zondervan Bible Publishers.

Library of Congress Cataloging-in-Publication Data

Martinson, Roland D., 1942-
  EFFECTIVE YOUTH MINISTRY.

  Bibliography: p.
  1. Church work with youth. I. Title.
BV4447.M336   1988   259'.2   88-6210
ISBN 0-8066-2311-X

Manufactured in the U.S.A.   APH 10-2030

            8   9   0   1   2   3   4   5   6   7   8   9

Contents

Preface

This book is born of struggle.

I struggled. As a bored—but seeking—teenager in a well-meaning, yet largely ineffective congregation, I struggled with the foundations of my faith. As a novice youth worker I struggled to be faithful to my calling with young people. I have struggled as a pastor, researcher, and educator to understand and expand the church's ministry with youth. With my wife Sherry I'm presently struggling to faithfully parent Terri, Timothy, Jonathan, and Kirk.

I'm grateful for the youth who struggled with me and the church throughout my 15 years of youth ministry. They provided enthusiasm, curiosity, honesty, idealism, and commitment which enabled their congregations to be more faithful ministers of the gospel of Jesus Christ. In a large measure this book belongs to Bonnie, Jim, Diane, Kent, Jennifer, and their friends.

This book also belongs to the dedicated adult leaders who were the "ministry family" I joined in sharing life and faith with young people. These persons became communities from which struggles with ministry issued forth in creative new beginnings.

During these struggles I have had youth ministry mentors. For four decades Dr. Merton Strommen has worked to provide accurate data upon which to build intentional ministry with youth. He has been my teacher and guide. Charles Peterson has given his life to young people on their pilgrimage into adulthood. Unabashedly Christian in word and deed, he was more than my coach—he was a guarantor, model, and spiritual father at a crucial stage in my adolescent faith struggle. Pastors Donald Ronning and Chester Johnson believed in me and gave me the freedom to experiment and develop new youth ministry strategies.

This book is also born of a particular perspective.

I am a white, middle-class, male Protestant. I grew up in rural America. My ministries have been in small-town, suburban, and urban settings in the midwestern and southwestern United States. The congregations I have served and the seminary where I teach are Lutheran, but I frequently speak to and lead workshops for youth leaders from other denominations, including Evangelicals. In my years of youth ministry I have worked with a number of female youth leaders, and they have influenced much that is written here. I have studied cross-cultural and international youth ministries.

This book reflects the bias of one with these life experiences. I make no apologies; I simply state their existence as I offer readers this new resource as part of the growing, significant stream of literature on ministry with youth.

Introduction

Youthfulness is a quality found to a greater or lesser degree in all of us. Honesty, openness, idealism, enthusiasm, and courage are qualities particularly present among adolescents. I believe young people can stimulate the exercise of these qualities within the larger church.

Youth and *young people* will be terms used to refer to early adolescents (10- to 14-year-olds) and late adolescents (15- to 18-year-olds). This focus has been deliberately chosen. The church has had difficulties ministering with these persons in the last two decades. A solid and rich tradition of faithful and effective youth ministry awaits broad application.

This book is written for anyone interested in competence in youth ministry. However, it is primarily addressed to a congregation's youth ministry representative (YMR)* and paid staff person or persons who are responsible for overseeing

---

*In this book I will use the term youth ministry representative (YMR) to refer to the member of a congregation who is not a paid staff member but who is responsible for overseeing youth ministry on behalf of the congregation. The YMR in a congregation will often be the person who chairs the youth committee, if such a committee exists.

youth ministry in that church and its community. Most often these persons will be a youth committee chairperson and the pastor. In some congregations they may be joined by a paid, lay youth worker. These two or three key leaders are encouraged to examine their congregation's youth ministry in light of this book's message. It is written to assist them in establishing a congregationally owned, indigenous youth ministry in their church.

In this book, five fundamental questions facing those ministering with youth are addressed:

Youth ministry—What is it?

Youth—Who are they?

Youth ministry—How will we do it?

Youth ministry—Who will do it?

Youth ministry—What will we do?

However, this is not only a theoretical inquiry into the nature of youth ministry. These questions are designed to be chronologically and systematically taken up as a congregation constructs or reconstructs its youth ministry. Used with the resources provided, this book could become a guide for renewing youth ministry in a congregation over a period of one to three years.

1

Youth Ministry Myths and Foundations

Youth ministry starts with an "intentional" theology. This means that perspectives and programs need to be constructed on the foundations of the Christian faith. The results of this construction will vary from tradition to tradition and church to church. Universal agreement is not the goal. The goal is a youth ministry shaped by the gospel as understood by one's own theological tradition and its interpretation of Scripture.

Pervasive myths with poor theological foundations have been barriers to effective ministry with youth. These myths are not necessarily consciously held, yet they distort youth ministry. They need to be identified and transformed into solid theological foundations.

Myth one presents youth ministry as the responsibility of the pastor or youth director or church member who is good with kids. This "Lone Ranger" myth is adopted by churches who believe they can pay or appoint one or two people to do youth ministry for them. The congregation abdicates its responsibility and sits back to judge how well the pastor, the youth director, or the youth sponsor is doing with youth.

This view of youth ministry centers in one leader and his

or her personality. At its worst, this myth leads to a personality cult. At its best, it makes ministry dependent on one person. Where this is the case, the congregation's youth ministry often "leaves" when that person leaves.

And leave they do. The overwhelming responsibility placed on one person is a large contributor to burnout among youth pastors and youth workers. They stay an average of only 18 months in their congregations. This "Lone Ranger" myth is largely to blame for volunteer youth and adult leaders becoming discouraged and bitter.

This myth often distorts the view pastors have of youth ministry. Because they are afraid of having the entire youth ministry shoved on them, they are led away from pastoral ministry with youth.

Foundation one: Youth ministry belongs to God through the ministry of God's whole church. Youth ministry is the responsibility of the *entire congregation* through its elected, appointed, and paid representatives. The pastor or pastors are to participate in youth ministry. Some churches will also call paid, lay youth workers to participate with the pastoral staff in youth ministry. A congregation needs to elect a person to supervise its ministry with youth. An elected or appointed group of the congregation's members can advocate, initiate, coordinate, and evaluate the congregation's youth ministry. Those who have the gifts can be appointed to do the hands-on work. The congregation as a whole needs to support the life and mission of youth in the church and the community.

This is not a pipe dream fit only for large congregations with big budgets. Almost every congregation where there are youth has a pastor and people who can join the pastor in guiding the congregation in ministry with young people. Youth ministry can be "owned and operated" by the congregation.

Myth two equates youth ministry with a congregational *youth group*. This myth is apparent in the response people most frequently give when asked about youth ministry in the congregation: "We have 10 or 25 or 75 who are active in our group." This view equates youth ministry with a specific set of programs. It suggests that only those youth involved in church activities are Christians. At its best, it equates ministry with programs and Christianity with specific church activity. At its worst, it becomes self-centered and exclusive. As the primary focus of youth ministry, the youth group approach mostly hinders rather than helps youth understand the life and mission of Jesus Christ's church in the world.

Foundation two: Rather than focus on the youth group, a church is to minister with *every youth in the congregation and reach out to other youth in the community.* Youth ministry focuses on persons. It works with the loner Christian as well as the gregarious Christian. It works with the rebellious Christian as well as the adaptive Christian. It reaches out to the growing number of unchurched youth in the community.

Steve was tall, skinny, and bright. He loved cars. He always had dirt under his fingernails and grease in his pores. His knowledge of engines provided him a part-time lawn mower repair job at Blake's Hardware. Steve rarely came to church and never came to youth activities. He was shy and reflective. "I guess you'd call me a loner," he said. On the third visit from his pastor, who stopped to chat with Steve in the back room at Blake's, Steve began to talk of his concern about one of his friends who was taking drugs. Six weeks later, Steve was instrumental in helping his pastor get his friend into treatment for chemical dependency. Steve never attended a youth group, yet he was an important part of the youth ministry of his church.

Myth three suggests that youth are the "future church" and youth ministry is preparing youth for adult church leadership. This myth misses the unique perspectives and gifts which youth can contribute to Christ's ministry. It mistakenly applies only adult perspectives to the Christian life. For some adults it provides an occasion to use Christian ministry to dominate and control young people.

Foundation three: Youth are not only the church of the

future; youth are a significant part of today's church. They have perspectives, enthusiasm, energy, and gifts which are crucial if Christ's ministry is to be inclusive, faithful, and effective. Most often young people are the finest musicians in a congregation. They've taken lessons long enough to be proficient; they're in practice; they love music. They can turn around the mood of worship with the sharp, bright sounds of a brass ensemble. The church needs the wisdom and gifts of the young as well as the old.

Myth four, popular during the late 60s and the 70s, claims that youth ministry is *no different* than ministry with other persons in the church. This point of view rightfully emphasizes that youth ministry must be integrated and not separated from the mainstream of the church's life and ministry. But it overlooks the fact that youth and their cultures are different than other age groups in the church. Youth is a life stage with its own questions, issues, and needs; youth cultures, even though they share much with the culture at large, have their own symbols and life patterns. Moreover, simply lumping a few youth together with large numbers of adults in the wider life and mission of the church does not take seriously the threat young people experience as a minority among an adult majority.

Foundation four: Rather than seeing youth ministry as no different, youth ministry can be understood as one of the many facets of life and mission of Jesus Christ's church. Youth ministry can emphasize both uniqueness and integration. It can explore the specific gifts and needs of youth and design ministries to tap these needs and gifts. It can integrate these diverse ministries with the overall ministry of the congregation.

Gary, age 16, stood at the door after the worship service. Without looking up from his shoes he said to his pastor: "You talked today about every Christian having a gift. I know mine. It's to be a driver." As he spoke, the mind of his pastor traveled to the parking lot and visualized Gary's '67 Chevelle with the orange axle, long pipes, and 454 cubic inch Oldsmobile engine. Gary continued, "You've been asking for someone to give elderly people rides to church." The pastor was uneasy. Here was someone who wanted to help, but who would ride with him? Suddenly the pastor remembered Clara. She was 73; her legs were crippled; her mind was sharp; her spirit tenacious and buoyant. She loved to come to church but couldn't drive. Wednesday after school Gary and the pastor went in the Chevelle to invite Clara to ride with Gary to church. And ride she did. They came together in style. She loved it. She loved him. She came to church, and, basking in her love, he grew and mellowed!

Myth five claims that youth ministry is a high congregational priority. If youth ministry is a high congregational priority, why aren't there more youth in attendance at worship? If youth aren't around, why aren't congregations more upset and involved in stemming their exodus? Sometimes leaders say: "We really care, we just don't know how!" Congregational leaders may be caring, yet one wonders why caring doesn't get translated into adequate personnel, relationships, support, activities, budgets, and facilities. An old proverb says: "One really only believes that which one actually does!"

Perhaps our ambiguity is most graphically reflected in the "youth coolie syndrome," in which a congregation hires a young, inexperienced college student or young adult to do their youth ministry for them.

It was Chuck, a young university student doing youth ministry in an urban congregation, who in his frustration used the term *youth coolie*. He defined what he meant with the exclamation: "They hire you for 20 hours per week, expect you to work 40, and pay you for 10! I'm a youth coolie!"

Foundation five: If a church is to do effective youth ministry, it must recognize the importance of youth ministry throughout the congregation and denomination. Youth ministry can actually be high priority. Congregations and denominations can acknowledge their need of youth's perspectives, enthusiasm, energy, gifts, and questions. They can rigorously respond to young people's need for the church during this crucial stage in life and faith development. They can honor the youth cul-ture's need to be influenced by the gospel. This commitment can be translated into prayer, thought, time, energy, people, events, budget, and facilities. A church can act, investing itself in young people's struggles and aspirations as well as inviting youth into those of the congregation.

Myth six suggests that youth ministry must be done by individuals who have youthfulness, charisma, and magic! This "pied piper" myth infers that those doing youth ministry must possess magnetic personalities that attract youth. Inherent in this concept is the notion that those who work with youth must be young, energetic, and filled with enthusiasm. This myth tempts congregations to adopt a pied piper approach or hire a young, inexperienced "youth coolie" to do their youth ministry for them. It excludes older persons in the congregation who have great gifts for youth ministry.

Foundation six: Youth ministry is best accomplished by young, middle-aged, and older persons working together. Youth ministry requires the gifts, diversity, and stability of a multigenerational network of people working as a team. The vast experience and the gifts given by the Spirit within the body of Christ are essential for faithful and effective youth ministry. People of diverse experiences, gifts, and needs can be identified and brought together for ministry with youth.

Myth seven: The history of primarily calling inexperienced and inadequately trained young people to do youth ministry reflects the myth that youth ministry is a beginner's job that does not require much education, experience, or skill. Nothing could be farther from the truth. Youth ministry is one of the most demanding ministries—so demanding and frustrating that many pastors and congregational leaders don't know what to do.

Foundation seven: Excellence in youth ministry requires persons of lively faith, solid theological understandings, sub-stantial relational skills, considerable organization ability, and maturity. Youth ministry requires competence. It is a challenging task that can be learned. It is worthy of aspiration and thorough preparation by our best youth and adult lay leadership as well as our best pastors.

Informed, skilled, and faithful youth ministry is possible. Churches have the people in their parishes. They have pastors. There are a growing number of full-time, professional youth workers. Most are men and women of ability and good will who can learn and develop the abilities needed.

Myths eight and nine: One of the debates today is whether or not youth ministry leadership belongs exclusively to youth from start to finish, or whether youth ministry must be led by adults who know what's good for youth.

Advocates of the "youth-only" position hold that if youth ministry is to be authentic it must come from and be carried out by youth. They suggest that adult involvement keeps young people from being open and honest. They claim it keeps youth from carrying out their ministries in their own way with their own people.

Advocates of the "adults" position hold that youth are irresponsible and unable to carry out what they ought to be doing in youth ministry. They suggest that a large part of youth ministry is passing on the tradition to the next generation; they see this to be the task of adult youth leaders.

Foundations eight and nine: Each of the above myths contains half truths. Youth must be principal participants in youth ministry leadership, and adults are needed. Both have vital gifts and necessary experience. Youth bring their honesty, enthusiasm, and talents. Adults bring their experience, stability, and resources.

The vital, delicate mix of youth and adult leadership can be developed. This youth/adult leadership mix has been effectively fostered in many churches through an action-reflection model of leadership training for youth, adults, professional lay leaders, and pastors. This model can be revived and others developed.

Myth ten: A final myth measures the effectiveness of youth ministry by the size of programs, the frequency of their activities, and the number of involved youth. Getting youth "active" or keeping them interested or hanging on to them are primary goals. In this program-oriented view of ministry, persons are often devalued and sometimes even overlooked. Resources are often wasted. Leaders are left confused, exhausted, and bitter. Youth and their families are harried and fragmented. Faith in Jesus Christ and the good news of the gospel can be lost in a whirl of activity or despair over its absence.

Foundation ten: Youth ministry that flows from the gospel is fundamentally person- and relationship-centered. The gospel focuses on Jesus Christ and his relationship to the world. God creates, renews, and sustains people and the world through relationships with them and their relationships with one another.

Youth ministry is relational. Young people respond most quickly to the gospel as it is transmitted through one-to-one relationships. When Jesus Christ's incarnation comes through the life of another, young people come to know God's love concretely and tangibly. Youth minister to one another best in relational arenas through which faith is transmitted and God's love is shared with others.

Youth ministry has a theological base even when that base is not consciously held. If that theological base is not deliberately reflected upon, it creates ministry in its own images which can become distorted myths. These myths point youth ministry toward wrong goals, produce shallow activities, and leave leaders frustrated and angry. Exploring theological foundations of these myths and their distortions of ministry is a first step in clearing the way for solid new foundations and effective youth ministry which is faithful to the gospel.

2

Theological Foundations
for Youth Ministry

A theological foundation for youth ministry can be grounded in the central message of the Scriptures and the Christian faith. This message can issue forth in mission and ministry, which are empowered by God's life-giving love in Jesus Christ.

The message

The life, death, and resurrection of Jesus Christ are God's decisive acts in history. In Christ we know God most clearly as the giver of life and truth. God creates the universe and all that it contains. The elements in all their combinations of inorganic and organic existence begin, continue, and end with God. God's gifts of consciousness, language, and meaning flow out of the past, through the present, and into the future. God establishes and sustains life and truth in all its mystery, splendor, and delicate harmony.

God gives life and truth again and again and again. When human beings and institutions distort and destroy, God reorients and renews. When human beings and institutions alienate and oppress, God reconciles and frees. God's gift of life continues toward full and abundant existence in Jesus Christ.

The world is the arena of God's awesome and mysterious life-giving activity. In Jesus Christ, God freely offers every single person truth, love, and freedom. Infants, children, adolescents, young adults, and middle- and old-aged persons of every place and time are to be the benefactors. Jesus Christ gave himself that every person might be free and become a gift to the world. Young men and women are to hear the message, live in it, and extend it in their own symbols, times, and places.

The message flows into mission

Jesus Christ calls persons into a community that is a sign of his continuing presence in the world. Members of this community are to experience in their individual and communal life the truth, love, and freedom God established in Jesus Christ. This community is to continue Jesus Christ's life-giving work. Its members are to be authentically human and freely participate in God's truth, love, and freedom in the world. Jesus Christ's life and mission lives on in them.

This ongoing ministry of Christ enlists all whom he has enlivened and called. Each person—every child, youth, and adult man or woman—has a unique place in the community's life and mission. Each person has need of the ministry of the community. Each person has a Spirit-given gift for the life of the community and its mission in the world.

Mission flows into ministry

The life and mission of the body of Christ most often take specific shape in Christ's church. Historically, the life and mission of that church have been called ministry. These activities of ministry are energized by God's Spirit and purpose; they enhance the life of the community and extend truth, love, and freedom in the world. They find their most succinct expression in the second chapter of Acts:

> God has raised this Jesus to life, and we are all witnesses of the fact. . . . They devoted themselves to the apostles' teaching and to the fellowship, to the breaking of bread and to prayer. . . . Selling their possessions and goods, they gave to anyone as he had need. Every day they continued to meet together in the temple courts. They broke bread in their homes and ate together with glad and sincere hearts, praising God and enjoying the favor of all the people.
>
> Acts 2:32, 42, 45-47

Luke describes the early church's ministry as: (1) *leitourgia* or worship, (2) *kerygma* or witness, (3) *didache* or teaching, (4) *koinonia* or communion, and (5) *diaconia* or serving those in need. Each of these tasks of ministry is developed and filled out in other parts of the biblical record and the Christian tradition. They have been renewing sources and guiding touchstones in the church. They continue to be so for youth ministers.

Youth ministry as worship

Worship is the intersection of God's past, present, and future activities. The Scriptures are not only read, but are interpreted as they interpret the times. The gathered community brings its multitudinous meanings, questions, and needs to be named and addressed. Individuals are healed and empowered by the presence, prayers, and songs of the entire congregation. At worship, those who are young and old, unique and diverse blend their presence and voices in unison.

Worship is the launching pad from which young people are propelled into life and mission in God's world. Instruction and inspiration are essential in times of complexity and despair. Forgiveness and reconciliation are crucial for youth who are alienated and lonely. Rhythms of rest and rigor, gathering and scattering, receiving and sending, being healed and healing are vital for those teenage saints called to be disciples of Jesus Christ.

Young people are too often separated from the rest of society. Education, athletics, and leisure activities herd them together with their peers—often like-minded peers from a very narrow slice of life. God's worshiping church is called to inclusivity. One form of youth ministry can be regular, inclusive, congregational worship with God's diverse people, who join their presence and voices around each other's leaders, languages, and concerns.

Youth ministry as witness

Ministry is proclaiming Jesus Christ as Lord! It is communicating in word, image, and action the life, death, and resurrection of Jesus Christ. To witness is to express to every person and nation in every generation the story of God's truth, love, and freedom.

> Evangelization is not a mere theoretical teaching about Christianity, but a sharing of the Christian experience, a testimony to the transforming interpersonal relationship brought about between man [woman] and God, and among men [women] by and in Jesus Christ. To tell another what one has seen, heard, touched and experienced is called bearing witness. That is what Christ asked of those men [women] who had experienced him. "You will be my witnesses not only in Jerusalem, but throughout Judea and Samaria and indeed to the ends of the earth." [1]

Youth ministry is preaching which not only reflects awareness of youth issues and struggles, but also addresses them in words and images young people understand. Media—faith-filled and beamed into young people's voracious appetites for sight and sound—get the story and significance of faith to youth in a form they can assimilate. Youth need faith-informed statements exploring and addressing the future of their earth, vocations, sexuality, values, and spirituality. Christian youth and adults can share their faith stories with one another; they can tell their faith stories to their friends, acquaintances, colleagues, and peers who do not know of God in Jesus Christ. The lives of Christian adolescents and young adults will be the only message many of their families, friends, schools, employers, and governments will hear and understand. Youth ministry can foster among young people the diverse forms and methods necessary to get out the good news.[2]

Youth ministry as teaching

Christian teaching is establishing the tradition, the living faith of God's people in each new generation. It is imparting information. It is guiding and reflecting. It is drawing out and exploring. It is testing and reformulating. It is confessing and reconfessing. God calls us to remembrance and awareness:

> O my people, hear my teaching; listen to the words of my mouth. I will open my mouth in parables, I will utter hidden things from of old—what we have heard and known, what our fathers have told us. We will not hide them from their children; we will tell the next generation the praiseworthy deeds of the LORD, his power, and the wonders he has done.
>
> Psalm 78:1-4

Learning is not one-directional, however. Teaching is also bringing seekers and tradition into mutual dialog. God has been at work; God is at work; God will be at work. Learning moves not only from past to present; not only from tradition to each new generation; not only from teacher to student; learning is mutual influence; it moves from the future and the present to rework the truths of the past. Each new generation is the bearer of God's continued commitment to the creation and God's new, creative work in the world.

The generations do not merely repeat and reproduce one another, nor does God expect them to do so. . . . History moves because God moves through it and generations are the vehicle of historical movement, the bearers of the new in the creative work of God. We in the church do not usually have a sufficient sense of expectancy in relation to the world and therefore do not have it in dealing with the younger generation. God is busy in his world; he is making new things under the sun. . . . The church thus should always approach the younger generation in this affirmative expectation, never with bewilderment or fear.[3]

Teaching is bringing the new creation, i.e., the gospel and its life-giving Word, Jesus Christ, into encounter and dialog with God's life-giving creativity in each new generation.[4]

Youth ministry as communion

To commune is to get to know another, to get involved in another's well-being, to commit oneself to another. Communion requires honesty, justice, and compassion. Communion is sustained by worship and prayer. Forgiveness is needed. Affirmation, confrontation, and consolation are necessary. Communion is establishing and sustaining life together.

This life together needs the presence of infants, children, adolescents, and young adults, as well as middle- and old-aged persons. Male and female, rich and poor persons of every race are important. Utilization of the Spirit's gifts in every adolescent and young adult is crucial for the church's life together. Young people's contributions to worship, education, witness, and community building not only significantly integrate them, but enrich the whole body's life and mission.

Youth ministry is administration which provides young people with just access to power—social, economic, political, and spiritual power in the congregation. Youth ministry is organization which appreciates the uniqueness of young people, yet promotes their integration with the rest of the congregation.

Youth ministry is people getting to know people. The

visitation of every youth in the congregation by adult youth ministry leaders is a direct way for a congregation to get to know and include its youth. At this stage in young people's faith lives, the church is most powerfully expressed through a caring person.[5]

Youth ministry as service

Jesus Christ announced the beginning and nature of his ministry by reading from Isaiah 61:

> The Spirit of the Lord is on me, because he has anointed me to preach good news to the poor. He has sent me to proclaim freedom for the prisoners and recovery of sight for the blind, to release the oppressed, to proclaim the year of the Lord's favor.
>
> Luke 4:18-19

Near the end of his ministry, Jesus spoke of his exalted role as Lord and Judge of history by pointing out his presence among those who are hungry, thirsty, rejected, naked, sick, or imprisoned. Jesus was very clear about his mission and that of his followers. He plunged into the pain and hurt of his followers and that of their brothers and sisters in the world. He cared. He noticed. He supported. He healed. He protested. He endured.

Youth ministry is servanthood. Adolescence and young adulthood are not a vacation from caring and responsibility. Youth ministry is not primarily an entertaining experience with refreshments. Jesus Christ calls both youth and adults to come, follow, and pick up their cross. Whatever one's age, to be baptized is to be commissioned to serve.

Adolescents and young adults spend a large amount of their time thinking about their identity; consequently they are often preoccupied with themselves. Some have inflated egos— our culture is narcissistic, encouraging most everyone to put themselves first. These realities make serving others particularly difficult for young people. To live for others is to go against the grain. Nevertheless the gospel calls young people to follow Jesus Christ, the "man for others."

Young people know of the struggles in their own lives and those of their peers. They're aware of the chemical abuse, sexual abuse, unwanted pregnancy, suicide, pressure, poverty, and family conflict experienced in their world. Adults have little access to adolescents and young adults facing these difficulties. Young people do. With some training and support, they can be a crucial part of the team of caregivers needed to bring healing and hope.

"What am I going to do when I grow up?" Every adolescent and young adult asks the question hundreds of times. It's a faith question as well as an economic and social question. To be a Christian is to have a vocation—the vocation of joining God as cocreator and recreator of this world. Checking out perspectives, work options, educational options, and immediate and intermediate life options in the light of this calling is integral to developing faithful and effective servants of Jesus Christ.[6]

Message, mission, and ministry

Youth ministry flows from the gospel message and mission as worship, witness, teaching, communion, and service. When it is grounded solidly in God's activity, youth ministry gains integrity, sustenance, and direction. The central question in youth ministry is: What is it? The central issues in this question are theological. They force us to wrestle with the fundamental understandings of our relationship with God, each other, ourselves, and the world. As these theological foundations are discovered and explored, they shape what the church does in youth ministry.

Today's youth culture also shapes today's youth ministry. Life situations with all their particularities need to be understood if youth ministry is to be substantive and significant.

The context of today's youth culture informs theological theory. There is always mutual influence. God's revelation flows from both theory and context. Therefore, faithful and effective youth ministry needs to focus on young people and their cultures. We turn there next.

3

Adolescent Physical and Intellectual Development

Young people are different from adults.

Among life's many seasons, none contains changes of greater breadth and mystery than adolescence and young adulthood. Bodies, minds, moods, meanings, and worlds expand with great speed and complexity. Not since infancy have the body and mind grown so rapidly. Never before have youth felt so different so quickly. Their worlds bring opportunities, decisions, and pressures and life-and-death dimensions. Theirs is the passage to full adult privilege and responsibility.

Adolescent development

In the past three decades, advances in the study of human development have expanded researchers' abilities to understand a growing human being's complex experiences. Research in physical and intellectual development has made the greatest advances and is widely accepted. Work on emotional and social theory has accelerated since the '60s. Recently, spiritual growth has received greater attention. Experts and their critics have emerged in each of these important spheres. Tracing all their work would be complex and beyond the scope of this book. The goal here is to glean the most important learnings from the developmentalists and draw implications for youth ministry.

Early and late adolescence are two distinct stages in human development. Growth occurs in general patterns for both sexes during these life stages. Some of those growth patterns begin in one of these stages and extend into the next. Therefore, these two stages of adolescent development will be considered together.

Physical development

The rapid physical changes in adolescence are called *puberty.*

For girls, puberty begins with breast development and the appearance of pubic hair as early as age nine or as late as age 14. Girls' rapid increase in height and widening of the hips begins as early as age 10 or as late as 15 and continues for two to three years. Girls may have their first menstrual period at age 10; almost all have had it by age 15. For the first two years, menstrual periods may be irregular. However, most girls are able to become pregnant when menstruation begins.

For boys, puberty begins with the enlargement of the testes sometime between the ages of 10 and 14. Approximately six months later the penis begins to grow and pubic hair appears. Boys begin a growth spurt about a year after they have started puberty, continue rapid growth for two years, and finish their growth more slowly over two more years. Boys produce mature sperm cells about a year after their testes have begun to enlarge. Generally the growth of facial hair and the deepening of the voice come toward the end of puberty, between the ages of 14 and 18.

Some physical changes are common to both boys and girls during puberty. Their faces and scalps become more oily. Acne and other skin problems are exacerbated by hormonal changes. Their developing sweat glands produce increased body odor.

Energy levels vary from great bursts to lethargy. They become awkward and clumsy during their most rapid growth periods.

The differences in physical change for boys and girls during puberty are many and significant. Girls begin earlier. Their growth spurt is earlier. Boys grow more rapidly once their growth spurt has begun and continue to grow longer. A ninth-grade girl may be nearly her full adult height and sexually mature. Her male, ninth-grade classmate may not have begun his adolescent growth spurt and may be just beginning to change sexually. At 14, one is a woman, the other a child.

Not only are there differences between boys and girls; great differences also occur among those of the same sex. There is great variation as to what happens during puberty. For example, puberty begins earlier for some boys and girls than others. Every girl and boy goes through these changes in their own way.

Implications for ministry

Many adolescents have difficulty adjusting to all the physical changes of puberty. They often don't understand what is happening within them. Their awareness of others and their need to measure up to societal standards make their physical changes distressing. They have mixed emotions about leaving childhood and becoming adults. Their dawning maturity raises questions of sexual adequacy. Physical development has great impact on their self-image and self-worth.

These physical changes and their impact point to specific ministries with early adolescent youth. Informing youth about puberty is helpful; conversations with trusted persons in which they can explore their concerns are even more helpful. Each adolescent needs personal affirmation—assurance that wherever he or she may be on the journey through puberty, it's OK. Gracious, accepting, individual and group relationships with peers and adults are immensely important during these changes. Skillful instruction and a sensitive, caring community of youth and adults are crucial ministries with adolescents.

Physical recreation, with cooperative as well as competitive goals, can be an exciting channel for cultivating and celebrating strength, stature, and skill. It provides a lively crucible for self-expression, cooperation, laughter, and conditioning.

One of the best ways to teach adolescents is through direct physical participation. For example, study of worship is helpful, observation of worship is more helpful, and active involvement in worship is most helpful. When adolescents sing, read, pray, and confess, they know, learn, and return to worship. What applies in teaching worship also applies in other areas.

Experiential education and clown ministry have made great contributions to expression and learning through physical activity. They have demonstrated that the sublime, the significant, and the spiritual are often most concretely known through mind and body joined in "doing." Canoe, bicycle, and backpack trips are individual and group physical activities that bring young people in contact with God's beautiful, mysterious, challenging earth. They are excellent modes for exploring creation, restoration, and communion.

Burgeoning physical strength, stature, and skill are gifts to be offered to God and neighbor. Walkathons, swimathons, etc. change physical energy into dollars for food and shelter for those of God's family caught in calamity. Young backs and arms can rake the lawns of those confined to wheelchairs; young brains and brawn can build or repair homes; young hearts and hands can care for children in church nurseries and after-school day-care centers.

Intellectual development

Much of the expansion of a person's intellectual capacities takes place during adolescence. About the time of puberty the brain undergoes a qualitative change which enables young people not only to learn more, but learn differently. An adolescent develops the capacity to conceptualize, analyze, and speculate.

The Swiss psychologist, Jean Piaget,[1] is the central figure in cognitive research. After carefully observing thought processes and IQs, Piaget noted that intelligence increased unevenly. Rather than developing steadily from one year to the next, he saw intelligence developing in spurts. Piaget called these spurts and their resultant intellectual capacities "cognitive stages." Each one of these stages of thought includes prior stages and makes them more sophisticated.

Piaget's stage three is the period of concrete-operations. Children ages 6 through 12 usually develop the capacity to think logically. They can observe, organize, and draw conclusions. They can memorize. Greater distinction is made between the imaginary and the empirical. The world revolves less around them. They can figure things out.

Stage four, the period of formal-operations, develops during adolescence. Most people begin this type of thinking between 11 and 15 years of age. They develop the ability to do abstract thinking, formulate theories, and speculate beyond themselves to others and the future. Questioning accepted truth, exploring complex constructs, and digging beneath the appearance of things all characterize this way of thinking. In this stage a person gains the ability to do both inductive and deductive reasoning. Although for most people these abilities appear during adolescence, some people never develop this type of thought.

Some of what Piaget and his followers have left us is suspect. In his schema, certain thinking is arbitrarily valued more highly. Intuition is given little attention. Too much of the work is male-biased. Great emphasis is put on progression, with little room allowed for regression. Yet Piaget's concept of qualitative changes in cognition occurring during human development is valid. His categories of types of thought, although altered, are widely used. His portrayal of adolescence as a qualitative cognitive shift toward abstract reasoning, idealism, introspection, empathy, and analysis has been well established.

Implications for ministry

Consciousness, language, and reason are vital gifts of God to be cultivated, consecrated, and celebrated. Understanding their role in human life and faith is vital for effective youth ministry.

The developmental shifts in cognition suggest that those seeking to enable others to internalize the Christian faith might well take note of what might be taught when and how. Cognitive development suggests that those working with adolescents need to coordinate their work with others working with children and adults. Much of the basic language and symbols of faith can be learned in early childhood. The data and stories of faith can be learned soon after. These children will learn best through immediate, concrete, empirical experience with the Christian tradition. During later childhood the details can be filled in and the tradition fleshed out through research, reading, and memorization.

Most adolescents have intellectual abilities beyond the childhood stages. Certainly they can learn facts; they want more, however. Most will accept the good news, but not before they've questioned, explored, and tested what they've heard. It is not enough to fill adolescent heads with facts. They need to probe and practice their learnings or they forget or become bored.

There is much in the Christian faith that must be understood and experienced if it is to be meaningful. A relationship with God is more of a guiding influence if it has been "owned" by the believer. Freedom, love, justice, trust, and hope must be understood and applied if they are going to be meaningful. A mature faith has to be reasoned and functional in life decisions if it is to be of any significance.

Ministry with adolescents affords them opportunities to explore the many aspects of faith, select those that are meaningful to them, reshape others to fit their own symbols, and integrate these complex dimensions of faith into their personal belief systems and life-styles.

Youth ministry draws on a wide variety of teaching methods within an inviting and safe learning environment in order to foster this expansive formation of faith. Young people's questions need to be honored and encouraged. Case studies, action-reflection-formulations, simulations, individual research, and socratic methods for learning are particularly effective with adolescents.

Youth ministry can afford the occasions for faith and life dialogs with peers, parents, community leaders, societal spokespersons, and their own heroes. The whole community is available for lively learning sites. It is possible to foster effective one-to-one and corporate learning climates. These climates are the catalytic environments in which young people risk examining and reformulating their fundamental convictions, values, morals, and beliefs.

Jesus was 12 years old when he was engrossed in conversation with the Jewish leaders in the Temple. Mary and Joseph found him "sitting among the teachers, listening to them and asking them questions. Everyone who heard him was amazed at his understanding and his answers. . . . And Jesus grew in wisdom and in stature and in favor with God and [human beings]" (Luke 2:46-47, 52). At age 12, Jesus was a developing adolescent thinker. His teachers had the good sense to take him seriously.

4

Adolescent Emotional and Social Development

Erik H. Erikson,[1] an American social-psychologist, is the central figure in adolescent developmental psychology. His work has been substantially revised and supplemented by the findings of more contemporary developmentalists, especially those of Carol Gilligan.[2]

Erikson postulated eight stages of human development. These stages normally take place during defined age spans and are focused in specific crises of the self. If these crises are constructively resolved, persons mature and develop strengths which enable them to cope with reality. Unresolved, these crises result in chaos and destruction. According to Erikson, each stage builds on those which have come before. Sometimes that which was resolved at a prior life stage must be reworked during the crisis of a later stage. It is possible for a person to stop maturing and even regress.

Erikson's schema of human development can be succinctly summarized using the categories of stage, period/age, achievements, and strengths.

Erikson's Eight Stages of Man[3]

Stage	Period/Age	Achievement	Strengths
1	Oral-sensory Infancy Years 0-2	Basic trust vs Mistrust	Drive and Hope
2	Muscular-anal Early childhood Years 2-5	Autonomy vs Shame/doubt	Self-control and Willpower
3	Locomotor-genital Middle childhood Years 5-8	Initiative vs Guilt	Direction and Purpose
4	Latency Later childhood Years 8-10	Industry vs Inferiority	Strategy and Competence
5	Puberty/Adolescence Youth Years 10-18	Identity vs Role Confusion	Devotion and Fidelity
6	Young adulthood Years 18-25	Intimacy vs Isolation	Affiliation and Love
7	Adulthood Years 25-55	Generativity vs Stagnation	Production and Care
8	Maturity Years 55-death	Ego Identity vs Despair	Renunciation and Wisdom

Carol Gilligan provides an essential critique of Erikson's work and a counterpoint to his view of human development. Drawing on her research with both women and men, she describes a different developmental process in women:

While for men identity precedes intimacy and generativity in the optimal cycle of human separation and attachment, for women these tasks seem instead to be fused. Intimacy goes along with identity, as the female comes to know herself, as she is known, through her relationships with others.[4]

Identity and intimacy are the key developmental issues in male and female adolescence and young adulthood. The answers to "Who am I?" and "Do I belong?" come together. Identity and intimacy come from many facets of experience and are multidimensional. During adolescence the struggle to resolve these questions is intense and focused in six dynamics.

Self-image: Although one might never suspect from the way some dress or act, adolescents are hypersensitive about their "image." Many even create an imaginary audience that they believe is observing and evaluating them and their behavior. Comments and responses are interpreted and shaped into a "self-portrait": "People say I'm cute; my teacher puts me down; peers avoid me; Betty smiled at me; my hair is too straight; I have pimples on my face; the basketball coach thinks I have potential." Day after day the creation of this composite inner portrait continues. Usually one or two attributes emerge as the unifying theme for the picture. The other dimensions fade into the background and organize themselves around those which stand out. This inner picture of how an adolescent sees herself is the central element in her self-identity.

This emerging self-image is more than just descriptive in nature. Adolescents judge the degree to which their personhoods are lovable, precious, and worthwhile. This judgment concerning self-worth is known as self-esteem. Self-esteem is made up of feelings about the self. All adolescents have a mix of good and bad feelings about themselves. All have the mix slanted either toward negative or positive feelings.

When self-esteem is positive in an adolescent, a cycle of positive reinforcement is created. Because the person feels worthwhile, he tends to see life in a positive light. Therefore, life and others approached confidently usually affirm the person, leading him to continue to feel good about himself. The opposite can also be true. In his classic study reported in *Five Cries of Youth* (Harper & Row, 1974), Merton Strommen discovered that 20% of teenagers surveyed lived a life of self-hatred. Society's images of the beautiful, popular, and vivacious teenager who is number one makes developing a positive self-image difficult. Adolescents are invited to compare and compete, and most must lose. Consequently, lack of adolescent self-esteem, often born of beginnings in a troubled family, is powerfully reinforced during this period of development.

Some adolescents have inflated self-images. These teenagers have an unrealistically high view of themselves; they are arrogant and overestimate their abilities, judgments, and place in society. In his book *The Inflated Self,* David Myer contended that adolescents' major problem is not inferiority but superiority. Myers reported the findings of a national survey of high school seniors who compared themselves to other people their age:

> Leadership ability—70% said they were above average; 2% said they were below average.
> Athletic ability—60% said they were above average; 6% said they were below average.
> Relational ability—60% said they were in the top 10%; 0% said they were below average.[5]

Because only half of a group can be above average, this study indicates (according to Myer) that at least a significant portion of the adolescent population see themselves more highly than they ought.

Two societal influences fan this inflated adolescent ego. Youth are admired and held up as the norm in American culture. To be young or youthful is desirable. Children want to be older; adults want to be younger. Americans' penchant for youthfulness sends unrealistic signals to some youth. The second influence is narcissism. Adolescents are bombarded with messages encouraging them to ask: "What's in it for me?" These self-biased messages lead many adolescents who already have inflated self-images to justify and further distort their place in the world.

Independence: Adolescent and young adult identity and intimacy are shaped from a history of dependency. As a child, the adolescent has been reliant on adults in many institutions. Mother, father, teacher, coach, doctor, and pastor have determined the child's world. Adolescence and young adulthood are a transition from being a "we" person to becoming an "I" as well as a "we" person. An adolescent wants freedom. She wants to go her own way, choose her own friends, and have her own thoughts. She holds things inside. She has secrets. Mobility is valued. Getting a driver's license and a car or having friends who have access to an automobile are high priorities. He wants to be capable of adult tasks. Dress becomes an expression of individuality and freedom of choice. Testing beliefs and values of significant adults is a way of clarifying his life-style. Self-awareness, self-reliance, confidence, and competence are the crucial components of independence. Individuation and connection are the goals. Trust of self and others are the key issues.

American culture both fosters and complicates adolescent independence. Our technological society not only gives youth a "moratorium" in which to be about the task, but also provides a rich and diverse teenage subculture from which to choose the symbols, relationships, and activities which are necessary for its accomplishment. There are permission, time, and means for testing, exploring, and maturing. On the other hand, amid great pressures to conform, compete, and succeed, contemporary adolescents are faced at earlier ages with life-determining decisions. Moreover, the complexity and uncertainty of the larger adult culture provide youth with overwhelming diversity and few models and opportunities to intentionally develop wisdom, competence, and responsibility.

Interdependence: "Do I belong?" is as fundamental to adolescent and young adult development as "Who am I?" Adolescent and young adult identity and intimacy are shaped in a crucible of interdependence. Adolescents and young adults must develop new life-support relationships with their families, friends, and the world.

Adolescents take a major step in leaving their parents as children in order to become adults and return to their families as mature kin. Moving out of one's childhood roles and relationships in the family is a complicated journey. New rules must be negotiated. Old patterns must be revised. Power shifts. Communication is strained. Conflicts must be resolved. Different needs call for satisfaction. Responsibilities for one another ebb and flow in uncharted directions. All these tasks call for more sophisticated interpersonal skills.

Separation or isolation from the family is not the goal of maturation. It usually is not even immediately desirable. Adolescents need the stability of their families as home base in their shifts in affiliation. Young people rework their support systems best in a network of long-term, loving, and honest family relationships. Working out identity over against or within a solid and respectful family of origin provides important coordinates and a safety net.

Peers become the staple of adolescent and young adult support networks. As adolescents and young adults renegotiate relationships with their families, friendships become crucial life-support systems. Having one or two or more friends with whom to "do things" is a life-and-death matter. Being accepted by one's peers is crucial for self-acceptance.

Mutual friendship is an art requiring great skill and wisdom. If adolescents and young adults learn and refine this art in peer groups, friendships, and romantic relationships, they find support and acceptance and feel secure. If not, there is isolation and rejection. Both have profound effects on identity and capacities for intimacy.

There is another network that adolescents and young

adults must negotiate as they establish their identity. Public officials, employers, colleagues, and law enforcement agents provide a parade of public persons with whom adolescents and young adults must work out life. Approaching these persons requires confidence and skill. The young person needs to develop new balances of self-care and responsibility in order to survive and have integrity.

Sexuality: The sexual unfolding and definition that occurs during adolescence is the greatest since fetal development and birth. Even though a person's gender is announced at birth and influences his or her childhood, adolescents must make their way through a sexual maze of anatomical, hormonal, emotional, and relational changes with their attending cultural, moral, and spiritual issues. What is a man? What is a woman? Am I heterosexual or homosexual? Am I attractive? How will I act? What do I do with all this energy? What if I get pregnant? What do I do with past sexual scars? These questions pervade the consciousness of adolescents and shape their identity and actions.

The sexual unfolding of adolescence is at the heart of identity and intimacy. Healthy acceptance—together with responsible expression—of an adolescent's sexuality gives definition and confidence to personhood as well as depth and tenderness to interaction with others. As boys accept their growth into manhood and girls their growth into womanhood, their self-confidence increases and their personalities are filled with new energy.

One's sexuality can be exploitive and destructive. Gender has been the basis for stereotyping women and men and oppressing both—particularly women. Sexual abuse destroys the foundations of intimacy and diminishes the identity of thousands of adolescents—especially women. Each year a million teenage pregnancies leave adolescents vulnerable and confused. "Faggot" or "queer" written on a school locker or shouted as one gets on a bus punches holes in an adolescent's self-portrait.

Competence: Much of self-image, independence, inter-dependence, and sexuality has to do with competence, with developing the skills necessary for living. Competence looms so large in adolescent and young adult development that it takes on a life of its own. To move from childhood to adulthood one must cope. A satisfying life in a complex society requires individual and relational courage.

Adolescent and young adult competence is pushed and measured at every turn. Intellectual and academic competence are presented as the ticket to rewards and power in the real world. Physical strength, coordination, and attractiveness are pictured as the road to happiness and success. Crucial decisions must be made about chemicals, sexual expression, family alignments, and vocation. Powerful, new, rapidly changing, and often contradictory emotions call for understanding, expression, and management. Most adolescents must be able to do well at school, be involved in extracurricular activities, work a job, spend time with their families, develop friendships, and have a good time. Others who live on the street must survive in a world where even their parents may not have made it. Success or failure in the fray determines and defines status, worth, and identity.

Purpose: Erik Erikson found that ideology played a significant role in forming adolescent identity. He saw a "universal psychological need for a system of ideas that provides a convincing world image."[6] Religion could play an important role in fulfilling this need by advocating prayer, developing basic trust, promoting faith, explaining evil, and supporting a collective sense of identity.

Adolescents and young adults have the experience and intellectual ability to wonder about their place in the scheme of things and to explore their roles in the web of human relationships. They question to discover that which they can accept. They test to determine whom they can trust. They probe to decide which way to go. The processes are not always visible or neat and ordered, but they are never far from the surface.

Most often the days and decisions of their lives force the issues. Will I cheat on the test? What will I do after high school? College? What do I do with my life? Do I look out for the other person? Do you play dirty to win? Should I have an abortion, keep the baby, or put it up for adoption? Will I continue to go to church? Should I kill myself? Is there anything to live for in a nuclear age? The faith, system of ideas, image of the world, and community of persons upon which young people draw to answer these questions become a layer of their identity as well as the glue which holds all the rest together.

Implications for ministry

The Scriptures are interested in humankind's questions: "Who am I?" and "Do I belong?" Identity and intimacy are fundamental elements of humankind's relationship with God. Personal identity and human relationships are directly influenced by faith. Our Christian tradition abounds with anthropological and sociological perspectives.

> What is man that you are mindful of him, the son of man that you care for him? . . . You made him ruler over the works of your hands; you put everything under his feet.
>
> Psalm 8:4, 6

> Love the Lord your God with all your heart and with all your soul and with all your mind. . . . Love your neighbor as yourself.
>
> Matthew 22:37, 39

Human beings have intrinsic uniqueness and worth. Each person is one of a kind. Every human being has her own physical, intellectual, emotional, social, and spiritual history. Never before has there been one like her; there is not another now; there never will be. Human beings are special editions. Human beings are valuable because they are rare, because they are multidimensional, because they are exceedingly capable, and because they have regal responsibility. Yet a person's essential worth comes from God, whose Spirit lives in every person. God is the source, restorer, and sustainer of all human life. Every person carries God's autograph, therefore every person has infinite worth.

Human life is fundamentally interdependent. Every person develops through an interconnected web of materials and persons issuing from God. Human existence rises and falls on the constructive or destructive qualities of human, societal, and global relationships. Respect, cooperation, and care between people and nations gives life. Malice, contention, and war between individuals and systems destroys life. People must learn that which works for the good of one within the good of all.

Ministry with youth grounded in these theological perspectives can be a significant force in adolescent identity and intimacy. God-given human uniqueness and worth can be effectively communicated to teenagers. Sermons can say this in symbols adolescents can understand. Songs can inspire as well as inform. Movies are able to set the notions to story. Affirming pastoral visitation, letters, and telephone contact turn the medium into the message. The perspectives of teen magazines, advertising, and much of the world of competitive sport can be critiqued and supplemented. Cooperative games that build on the gifts of every participant are a healthy addition to those which are designed for the initiated few. The strengths of every adolescent in the congregation are gifts of the Spirit which not only build up the body of Christ, but if tapped, adorn the spirit of the possessor. Youth ministers can foster an adolescent-adult church community where the ways of relating are affirmation, cooperation, respect, sensitivity, confrontation, and forgiveness rather than contention, competition, cutting, manipulation, and division. Parents of teenagers can be provided perspectives and methods for effective work with their adolescent or young adult. A Christian congregation can be a lively crucible for shaping teenage identity in solid, healthy images drawn from faith!

Youth ministry can also assist adolescents struggling with inflated self-images. The Christian faith has a solid understanding of pride's destructive role in individual and corporate life. The cross and the empty tomb with their empowering grace and hope proved the focus:

> Christian faith proclaims something more significant than psychological adjustment. Its hope is not on a make-believe image of human nature, nor does it promise relief from life's agonies. We need neither deny our propensity of selfishness, pride and illusion, nor wallow in it. The good news of the resurrection faith is that human evil will not have the last word. Our valuing of ourselves can be anchored in something more substantial and lasting than the shaky ground of our own virtue and wisdom. Our vision of a new age to come gives hope and direction to our life here on earth.[7]

Participation in a lively Christian community can provide youth with the support to form their own personal faith and worldview. Basic faith propositions can be explored intellectually and experientially. Contemporary issues and events can be addressed concretely and theologically. Vocational futures loom large and call for research, resourcing, and decision. There are immediate decisions regarding chemicals, sexual expression, time, family, employers, friends, freedom, power, and money. Each of these invites consideration. All have faith dimensions and provide occasions for significant, one-to-one and group ministry. Every adolescent's accumulated responses to these issues forge his self-image, independence, interdependence, sexuality, competence, and purpose.

The church is in a unique position from which to pursue a no-subject-barred approach to sexuality. Youth ministry can bolster parental confidence, knowledge, and participation in guiding teenagers into sexual maturity. Facts, life-styles, attitudes, values, and beliefs can all be addressed and explored at church. Communication among peers, the sexes, and adolescents and parents can be fostered. Support can be developed for those who make decisions that run counter to prevailing peer or adult standards. Forgiveness, acceptance, and new beginnings are gifts in the church that are vital to those who have made bad choices or have been abused.

Life together as the people of God provides an extended family of faith in which adolescents can work out identity and intimacy, balancing care of self with care of others. In the Christian faith there are perspectives that inform these balances. The gospel provides love, forgiveness, and hope when rejection, abuse, and narcissism destroy. Interpersonal and group relationships fostered by the freedom, truth, and love of Jesus Christ provide a laboratory and safety net in which to work out the sensitivities and responsibilities of intimacy. Christian brothers and sisters in the next chairs and around the world are a matrix within which to learn to value one's own life and that of every person in the world.

Sarah was average. So said her "yardsticks"—her report card, her swimming stats, her physical measurements. So said her teachers, coaches, and peers. But average was not acceptable to her parents. They expected superior, excellent— the best. Her father was a doctor; her mother a socialite. Sarah was not measuring up. She knew it.

Sarah worked at measuring up. She studied long and hard. She "fixed herself up" and "dressed preppy." She was always on a diet; she ate very little or binged and threw up. It was never enough.

Her pastor met her for Saturday lunch at McDonald's. Sarah's spirit was heavy, melancholic. Although she never mentioned suicide, her language was self-destructive. She negatively compared herself to her sister, who two years before had been valedictorian. She compared herself to her best friend, who was that year's homecoming queen. She compared herself to her childhood playmate, who had become a basketball star.

Sarah's conversation with her pastor set her off on a long journey. There were more tough and tender talks. She began participating in a peer Bible study and support group at church.

First she joined, and then led, the liturgical dance troupe during worship. There were hard days of individual and family therapy. A summer of work among poverty-stricken children in Appalachia took her mind off herself and sparked her capacities to lead and nurture. A year at college among new friends in campus ministry provided a new start and an affirming family of faith. Two specialized education classes confirmed and broadened her abilities to work with mentally handicapped children. An accident on a backpack trip she led in the wilderness tapped courage, stamina, and wisdom she never knew she possessed.

Sarah graduated from college at 23, in about the middle of her class. But she was not average. So said the children she had taught, the man whose life she had saved in the wilderness, and the camp board that hired her to be their first female director. So said the twinkle in Sarah's eye. Sarah was Sarah—tough, tender, compassionate, and creatively Sarah. Sarah was unique and valuable. She knew it. She wrote her pastor to tell him so—and thank him and the church for believing it long before she did!

5

Adolescent Faith
and Moral Development

James Fowler has pioneered the study of faith development.[1] Relying heavily on the work of Piaget and Erikson, Fowler has followed faith as an integral part of human maturation. Fowler defines faith as underlying patterns of thinking and feeling which inform a person's life and guide his or her behavior. Fowler is more concerned about how one believes than what one believes. He sees faith as a way of giving purpose to one's life and therefore as a universal human enterprise. Fowler writes: "Faith is an active mode of being and committing, a way of moving into and giving shape to our experience of life. . . faith is always relational; there is always another in faith."[2] For Fowler the opposite of faith is meaninglessness and loneliness.

Fowler describes faith's unfolding in six stages, three of which are germane to adolescent development.

During stage two, mythical-literal faith, children ages 6-11 draw on the faith of others to organize their world. They investigate the faith of parents, pastors, teachers, and heroes who are their sources of authority. These children can separate fantasy from fact. Rituals, symbols, pictures, and music are important vehicles for receiving and expressing faith. Stories integrate their experiences and beliefs. Beliefs and values are interpreted literally and usually accepted without question. God is still pictured in human form. There is usually a very simple and consistent view of the world.

Stage three, synthetic-conventional faith, usually begins during early adolescence. This stage is dependent on the individual's capacity to think abstractly. The adolescent possesses the capacity to discern the complexity of his world. He can struggle with contradictions and their divergence from his own beliefs. Choices are delineated. Decisions regarding direction and behavior are made. A supportive group of like-minded believers is crucial. Opportunities to act out beliefs are important for testing their validity and expressing commitment. God is seen in relational terms, most often as a loving friend or angry judge.

During stage four, individual-reflective faith, late adolescents and young adults age 18 and older, not only critically examine their beliefs, but also reflect on how these beliefs have been formed. Because of increased capacities for self-reflection and abstract thinking and their journeys toward self-reliance, these persons struggle to construct systems of belief that square with their perception of reality and are free from hypocrisy and contradiction.

Most adolescents move from stage two through stage three to stage four. Many people never move to the complex stages. Some develop no further than stage three. Few people move beyond stage four. The journey of faith moves like an upward spiral. The stages flow and are open-ended. The higher stages are more desirable. Yet Fowler writes: "Each stage has the potential for wholeness, grace and integrity and for strengths sufficient for either life's blows or blessings."[3]

Even though there are important changes in the quality and expression of belief, high levels of faith commitment continue during adolescence. The Princeton Religious Research

Center's study reported on their findings from a selected sample of American adolescents:

95% believe in God.

85% pray.

75% believe in a personal God.

52% say grace before meals.

On the other hand:

67% said institutional religion does not reach out to them.

60% said organized religion is not an important part of their lives.[4]

A study conducted by Merton Strommen through Search Institute in 1980–1984 indicated that a majority of young adolescents found faith to be the most important or one of the most important influences in their lives.[5]

Each of these studies indicates that faith in God continues for most adolescents even though it takes individual expressions which more often than not do not include participation in organized religion.

Faith plays an important role in adolescent and young adult development. Adolescence is a time of idealism, enthusiasm, and curiosity. It is a time of growing interdependence with God and other human beings that calls for commitment—commitment which springs from intellectual, emotional, and physical needs for people, beliefs, values, and decisions. A lively faith enables adolescents to make this commitment and formulate a philosophy of life that flows from an allegiance to God.

Moral development

Lawrence Kohlberg, a Harvard University psychologist, has conducted research on moral development.[6] Focusing primarily on moral reasoning, he has discovered differences in the ethical thinking of children, adolescents, and adults. Kohlberg is interested in why people reason as they do, as well as the conclusions to which they come. He contends that people go through predictable levels of moral reasoning in a fixed sequence.

Kohlberg measured moral reasoning using responses to three issues: justice, empathy, and the value of human life. On the basis of these responses he postulated three levels, two of which are germane to adolescent development.

The conventional level of moral reasoning usually begins at age 10 and continues until 16. Approval is the key principle. One does what makes one a nice person in the eyes of others. Conformity to peer expectations sets the norm. Intention and sincerity are influences. Fixed rules inform decisions. One must obey outside authority. Laws, rules, and traditions portray what is moral.

The post-conventional level usually begins between the ages of 14 and 16. Personal convictions and universal principles mark moral reasoning at this level. Accepted laws and rules are questioned as individuals work out moral principles based on their own convictions rather than outside authority. Morality, laws, and society are to serve persons. Mutual good and responsibility are to inform one's personal convictions. No one is better than anyone else. One must not violate one's conscience.

Implications for youth ministry

Faith and moral formation are at the heart of the mission of the church. The church exists to proclaim God's presence, to nurture one's relationship with God, and to shape one's life in God's truth and love. Through the church God uses Scripture, prayer, Baptism, and the Lord's Supper to initiate and sustain faith as well as form values.

In a book on religious education, Ronald Goldman has articulated adolescent needs that he believes should be the church's "first concern."[7] His description of the needs the church must address with adolescents depicts key goals for faith and moral formation. The five goals Goldman cites are security in freedom, significance and status, idealism and altruism, love, and meaning for life.

In *Five Cries of Youth,* a book on the lives of mid- and late-adolescents, Merton Strommen[8] found five concerns which he portrayed as "cries." Those five concerns were: self-worth, family unity, human welfare, God's favor, and personal faith. He portrayed them as: the cry of self-hatred, the cry of psychological orphans, the cry of social protest, the cry of the prejudiced, and the cry of the joyous.

The work of Fowler, Kohlberg, Goldman, and Strommen suggests five areas where youth ministry might make contributions to the faith and moral formation of youth.

Celebration of the awesome

Adolescents seek symbols that represent the hopes and dreams of their expanding world. They search for movements which concretely focus their beliefs and needs. Some chase experiences that stretch the boundaries of their imagination and consciousness. They look outside themselves for heroes and art forms which represent truth, power, and love. Broadened sensitivities, deepened comprehension, and new enthusiasm provide them with great capacities for commitment and adoration. Shifting worlds, expanding responsibilities, and unfolding needs push them to reach out for security and direction.

Adolescents and young adults will seek and respond to "God figures" and "holy events" in shapes and forms they can appropriate. Athletes, automobiles, musicians, and actors and actresses are found on posters in millions of teenage bedrooms. These are joined by teachers and coaches as tangible expressions of their adoration and needs. Videos, concerts, and athletic contests provide occasions and channels for their enthusiastic participation. Each teenage generation invents jargon to express its attraction to the ultimate, supreme, and transcendent.

Adolescents tend to see God as close friend—as a faithful,

understanding, and reliable close friend. Individually and internally, they are immanently spiritual. Youth ministry can provide them with lively symbols and timely occasions for worship. Their experience, music, and symbols can be tapped for expressions of their appreciation and need of God's ultimate friendship and much more. Most often young people's fresh expressions can be an enriching part of the worship experience of the entire congregation. There will need to be youth worship services of great variety in size, location, and occasion.

Meaning for life

This generation of youth has had little time to assimilate the rapid changes around it. Space travel, the threat of nuclear holocaust, abortion, global media coverage, world hunger, advances in medicine, and cultural pluralism provide youth with a dizzying array of challenges and possibilities. These scientific and cultural changes challenge faith and morality; reconciling them with personal beliefs and values is difficult yet they call for response.

Youth ministry can foster guided discussion of these issues. Fascinating video presentations can graphically place the issues before young people. Group and one-to-one discussions are arenas for exploring them in the light of the Christian faith. Knowledgeable individuals are available to tell their stories, share their experience, and present alternatives. Vehicles exist for concerted action. Goldman says, "A great deal of time must be given to an exploration of the validity of differing ways of arriving at the truth."[9] Among these can be the lively approaches of the best—past and contemporary—Christian thinkers. This means getting the "faith story" of God's life-transforming participation with humankind, Israel, and the church freshly retold among young people. Adolescents and young adults are capable of reality-oriented, integrated faith. Getting involved with their questions in light of the faith of the past and present fosters wisdom and hope.

Freedom within security

Adolescents and young adults live in a pressured world of high risk. Some teenagers say their teachers and coaches have labeled them successes or failures by the time they are halfway through middle or junior high school. As they are being asked to prove themselves, they are loosening family ties and looking to delicate peer relationships for support. The marriages of 40% of their parents' are breaking up. Simultaneously they are moving away from old restrictions, testing new ways of behavior, and facing an ever-expanding world of responsibility.

The church can provide freedom and security for this adolescent and young adult journey. Youth ministries can supply caring adults whose friendly acceptance provides adolescents with security and opportunity for independence. Erik Erikson called these people "adult guarantors." He saw them as key adult figures who were not in a position of direct authority, but who could be trusted; he saw them as life-guides on the adolescent road to maturity. An adult guarantor is someone to talk to; who listens more than speaks; who is tolerant and nonjudgmental; whose authority and respect lie in maturity and genuine interest. At this age, adolescents and young adults often see adult guarantors as God figures—men or women whose characters reflect the God who is a wise and trusted friend.

Adolescent and adult church communities can develop life together where teenagers find a spiritual family. Firmness, honesty, compassion, respect, and forgiveness are relational dynamics that bring grace to young people's experience. Built into the patterns of group life, these dynamics of the gospel form a solid, life-giving community—a secure place for youth to belong and to exercise their independence.

Idealism and service

Adolescent and young adult intelligence and sensitivity heighten their perceptions of injustice and hypocrisy. These same capacities often provide them with a vision of a better world. Because they do not yet have great economic and family responsibilities, they are more free to advocate and work toward change and social welfare. They have a unique vantage point from which to criticize, to be different, to go and serve.

By harnessing the power of the gospel with the humility and compassion of those adolescents who are idealistic and altruistic, the church can provide a ministry to their peers. The message of the cross is a call to take on those who believe the world revolves around their whims and desires.

Jesus Christ was a compassionate, radical idealist. Youth ministry might well lift him, his words, and his actions before adolescents and young adults. He stands ready to be their leader. His life and ministry can give their idealism direction. He comes to join and strengthen them in their dreaming and work. He will pick them up when they and their dreams are bruised and battered.

Worth and values

The formation of life-affirming values is directly related to love of self and others. If an adolescent or young adult does not value herself and others, she will act destructively toward both. When love of self and others exists, one can move on to teach and clarify values that promote life and respect property.

Youth ministry can proclaim and foster the God-endowed uniqueness and worth of every human being. This task is at the heart of gospel ministry. From this creative and redemptive affirmation of human worth follows youth ministry's responsibilities for moral formation. The church needs to engage adolescents and young adults in exploring what shape their gratitude for God's grace might take in every time and place. What is good and right and beautiful? What approaches do Christians take in making decisions about tough, complicated issues? How does one balance self-care with responsibility for others? What is God's will? What is our response to the gospel? These questions can be asked universally and particularly. Not many parents and community leaders are assisting adolescents and young adults in developing a consciously moral, intentionally value-based approach to life; youth ministry can help meet this need.

6

Youth Cultures

The culture of American youth is one of their orienting "locations," exerting powerful influence on their lives. To understand this culture is to understand something of every young person. The institutions, symbols, and dynamics of this culture must be addressed if youth ministry is to have public as well as personal impact.

Contemporary youth culture

What is today's American youth culture like?

It is extensive. It includes early adolescents, late adolescents, and young adults. Persons ages 10 through 25 are shaped by its influences. Better nutrition and preventive medicine have lowered the age at which puberty begins; a technocratic, complex society requires greater preparation and a longer entrance process. Those two factors mean 15-plus years of tentative, disengaged waiting on the fringes of society. It marks a long period of paradoxical freedoms and economic dependence. There are tough questions about sexual expression and commitment. Many youth feel dislocated with no place to call home. There is little stability, with frequent changes in community, living quarters, friends, classmates, and employment.

Not many significant work responsibilities exist whereby youth can shape their identities through contributions to the larger culture. American youth culture circumscribes millions of adolescents and young adults who exist in a long period of great transition.

Today's American youth culture is pluralistic. Persons of many races and religions gather on most high school and college campuses. People of both sexes, many races, and a variety of life-styles provide the music and movies of the younger generation. Youth themselves have diverse interests, values, and life-styles. Often this diversity creates vested interest groups and polarity. There are cliques and gangs. Very clear economic class distinctions are developing with growing numbers of poor and wealthy youth. Contrasting ideologies abound among young people. Almost anything goes in dress and hair style. As long as one is free to have one's own views, there is a high level of toleration for and acceptance of differing views and ways of life. There is a dizzying array of influences and options bombarding most youth.

Today's American youth culture is individualistic and privatistic. Most youth narrowly focus on their personal world. They are primarily concerned about developing a happy marriage, friendships, a career, and a comfortable life. They want to get ahead. Law and order, education, and a good job are valued for this reason. Most think their lives will be better in the next few years; at the same time they see the nation and world deteriorating. They exhibit little interest in improving the community, nation, and world.

Today's American youth culture is consumer-oriented. Adolescents possess great amounts of discretionary income. A vast majority have part-time jobs. Many have basic living expenses provided by parents so that their income is spent on snack foods, beverages, clothes, records, tapes, stereos, videos, recreation, cars, and travel. Consequently, young people are the target of ambitious advertising campaigns and constant changes in fashion. Identity and worth are shaped by what you wear or own or drive. Life becomes a pressure-cooker for those who work long hours at minimum wage jobs so that they can have money to buy and ski or surf. For others, such as large numbers of Black and Mexican Americans, it means the frustration of being locked out and jobless. Many youth choose to take the high risk of dealing drugs to be a part of the consumer world. Some rural youth cannot participate in this consumer-oriented culture because they work with their parents to break even in family farming.

Today's American youth culture is relationally impoverished. Over one-third of American teenagers have experienced their parents' divorce. Most of these have participated with one or both of their parents in new, blended families. Many have two parents, two step-parents, and siblings as well as step-siblings in their own families. These teenagers often move back and forth between families on weekends and vacations. Participating in these changes can be enriching for adolescents; however, most of the research indicates that youth in these situations are hurt and confused and tend to withdraw from significant participation in their relationships. Many American adolescents live in homes where there has been and still is little time for relationships with their distant grandparents, working parents, siblings, or day-care attendants. They have little experience with relational stability and intimacy; they've had little parenting from anyone. Peer friendships, often fast-changing and short-lived, are their major relational base. Volatile, burgeoning sexual relationships are sought for support and nurture. There have been few adults in their local neighborhood with whom to create community. A large percentage of American adolescents say they feel isolated and are lonely. Many believe this relational fragmentation is the reason teenagers list satisfying marriage and good friendships as their highest priorities.

There is a new view of women in today's American youth culture. Large numbers of female adolescents are participants in interscholastic and recreational sports. Three-fourths of all college women emphatically list career development to be their number one goal. Teenage girls see their mothers and sisters gaining greater access to a world that once belonged to men. Young women are developing their intellectual abilities and physical strength in preparation for full participation in every aspect of public life. This does not mean that female adolescents are disinterested in marriage and family; most anticipate marriage and bearing one or two children. Nor does the changing view of women mean there is a new view of men. Young men have not changed nearly as much as their female counterparts. A few see themselves with larger roles in domestic and childrearing responsibilities; some are developing their empathetic, intuitive, and caregiving side; yet these remain a minority. For the most part, it is women who have joined men in *their* world.

Today's American youth culture has an electronic consciousness. The "box," a large, portable stereo, has become a symbol of their culture. A portable stereo with earphones has become a constant companion of many. Theirs is a world of stimulation; sound and sight are nearly constant extensions of their awareness. Consequently, most have become multimodal. Listening to the stereo while studying is a must for many. Simultaneously listening to the stereo, watching television, and studying are possible and even comfortable. Silence and solitude are unbearable. Computers and their close companions, video games, are old friends. Young people thrive on intense visual and audio stimulation.

The threat of destruction of life on the planet is a significant element in the subconscious of American adolescents. The vast majority are aware of living in an era of the potential destruction of the human race. They know the threat is real; many believe it will come in their lifetimes.

American youth culture today is fast-paced and pressured. Most adolescents live in the fast lane. Many attend classes, study, work part-time jobs, participate in extracurricular activities, and have significant recreational involvements. Some, particularly Black youth, can find no work, are disinterested in school, yet end up living in the tensions of the street, pressing for that which the more affluent already have. American adolescents must catch up to the previous generation academically; some must catch up to white, upper- and middle-class students in good schools. All must get good grades so they can get a good job. Adolescents must become mature and responsible early; yet they are allowed neither to have adult responsibilities nor to grow up too fast. They must know how to handle their parents. Crucial decisions must be made again and again about use of drugs, sexual activity, and friendships. Looking good is essential for acceptance. Communication and social skills must be developed in a world that revolves around establishing and reestablishing relationships. They must work their way through college. They must have a good time. The "musts" seem to never end. Drugs, anorexia, destructive forms of sexual expression, and suicide become the way out for many.

Today's American youth culture is less influential than that of a decade ago. The small numbers of youth coupled with the growing numbers of persons over 65 and the bulge in the population at 30 have made American youth of today much less powerful. Even though they still have large amounts of discretionary income, at present they are not needed for an ongoing war as was true 15 years ago. The privatistic focus of their lives diminishes their public impact. By and large, they work at nonunion, minimum wage jobs. Most can't vote.

American youth culture today includes large numbers of adolescents and young adults who are deeply wounded. Suicide has increased 300% in a generation. Automobile accidents, particularly alcohol-related automobile accidents, kill tens of thousands. One-fourth will be chemically dependent by age 25. One of four young women will have been sexually abused; more will have been sexually exploited. More than one million teenage women are becoming pregnant each year; many have abortions about which they are uncertain and are left confused and guilty; others keep their babies and struggle in poverty to find their way to adulthood. Nearly one in five adolescent and young adult women will become anorexic. Hundreds of young men will die or enter the criminal system through gang warfare, drug trafficking, and robbery. It's not a pretty picture, but it's real. For many youth, it means life ends or is permanently scarred just as it begins. For society there are horrendous losses and costs.

Today's American youth are gifted. They possess breadth of experience and great native intelligence. They are physically more healthy than any other generation. There are greater opportunities, especially for women and minorities. Youth are energetic, hardworking, and purposeful. The generations before have taught them the importance of both vision and limits. They have tremendous educational, economic, social, and spiritual resources. The perspectives and capabilities of women are being more fully appreciated and realized. Global economics, communication, and potential destruction provide them with the specter and necessity of international negotiation and justice. They are marrying later; most are becoming more intentional about both marriage and family. Many are becoming independent thinkers, using their unique perspectives to forge new models for personal and institutional life. They possess the consciousness and capabilities to make great contributions to the common good.[1]

The church has a unique challenge with American youth and their culture. Youth ministers can ask: "Where is God at work here? What is God saying to all God's people through these young people?" Persons in youth ministry have the opportunity to respond to young people's crucial and significant questions and issues. Gifted young men and women await the sweet words of the gospel and the challenges of Christ's life and mission in the world.

Youth in each community and church

The young people of each church and community are peculiar to their time and place. Even though they share to some extent the adolescent developmental journey and the American youth culture with all other youth in the country, youth in each congregation and community have a life that is uniquely their own. Knowing these youth and their world is crucial to faithful and effective youth ministry.

A variety of effective approaches are available for acquainting oneself with local youth and their culture. Field studies and psycho-social surveys are the most popular. Field studies and surveys[2] get at the unique nature of youth in each church and community. They are channels to the entire church for God's truth and work among youth. They read God's ongoing revelation in a new generation. Taking seriously studies and surveys and their findings provides clear focus for congregational youth ministry and taps the Spirit's gifts in the teenage saints for the mission of the church.

Each young person

Adolescent developmental studies are helpful to those doing youth ministry. Understanding the American youth culture is important. Discovering the youth subcultures of each congregation and community is crucial. However, the only way to genuinely know each young person is to respectfully enter his or her life. If youth ministry is nothing else, it is visitation. There is no better way to enter her life than meeting her in her world and listening carefully to her story. There is no better way to discover God's revelation through a young person's life than sharing his pathos. There is no better way to participate in God's ministry to him than personally joining him in receiving and responding to the gospel.

Attending to the life of a young person is a difficult, demanding art. Respectful entrance to another person's world cannot be quickly programmed or accomplished cheaply. One must be genuinely interested; patient, careful listening is required. It takes time for trusting relationships to develop and for lives to unfold. Personal commitment and willingness to get involved are demanded; skills in affirmation and confrontation are necessary. There are risks. One must recognize and respect personal boundaries. Sharing faith and life in mutual conversation brings surprises and sometimes exhaustion.

In spite of the demands and risks, visitation with young people can be learned and accomplished in every congregation. Pastors, youth workers, adult youth ministry leaders, and young people can all do it. Pastors must do it. Together with formulating inclusive worship and preaching about that which is significant to youth, visitation with youth is a nonnegotiable pastoral responsibility. Lay people with relational aptitudes and interests can be recruited and trained to join in this ministry.

Young people are no different from others; yet they are unlike anyone else. Something of their experience is portrayed in developmental studies. Much of their world can be found in American youth culture. More of their life is discovered in their particular time and place. Most of their revelation of God and needs for ministry are encountered as one meets them. The church can significantly join them in their life's journey. The ministry of organizing a congregation so that it can join them in that journey calls for careful attention. We turn there next.

7

Organizing
for Youth Ministry

Youth ministry is a congregational enterprise. Every young person is a part of it. The congregation's elected officers or elders have significant roles. Worship leaders, teachers, and custodians are involved. There are needs for advocates for youth on committees who call pastors and plan budgets. Adult persons who affirm the presence of youth at worship and remember them in their prayers have a place. Young people who sing, play instruments, and assist in other ways during the service bring vitality to the congregation's worship. Some youth may be needed to drive the elderly to church or rake their yards or visit them when they are shut in. Other teenagers might care for infants, teach Sunday school, and reach out to their peers. Some young people will join adults in working for justice in the community, nation, and world. Youth ministry is an integral part of the ongoing life and mission of the entire congregation. How can the entire congregation do youth ministry?

Administration

A congregation is a local expression of the people of God that functions like a human body. Every human body has a central nervous system. Every central nervous system has a brain and a spinal cord with particular functions. Every brain or spinal cord is made of cells which carry out its work.

Administration is the central nervous system of a congregation. It is one of the gifts of the Holy Spirit to the church to build up the people of God and carry on the work of ministry. Administration is a gift for ordering the life and mission of the entire congregation. Administration is a gift to groups of persons with particular functions in the congregation. Administration is most specifically a gift to individuals who oversee a congregation's ministry.

Faithful and effective youth ministry is grounded in quality administration. It is through careful administration that the fundamental theological questions of the purpose and direction of youth ministry can be raised. Unless there is effective administration, a very few persons end up doing youth ministry and the rich gifts of the congregation are left untapped. Without competent administration there is little or no communication, coordination, or cooperation, and youth ministry becomes destroyed, fragmented, and divisive. Administration can enable power to flow justly so that youth are not forgotten or manipulated marginals in the church.

Staff and congregational representatives

Every congregation has two distinct lines of administration. The nonstaff representatives of the congregation make up the first line. These are people charged to use their gifts to coordinate the life and mission of the congregation. These persons focus and channel the power and responsibilities of the church in its varied tasks. They are the primary manifestation of the congregation's ministry of administration. The pastor and other staff are the second manifestation. Every pastor's call contains provision for supervision. Christian education directors, parish workers, and youth ministry staff associates often have administration as a part of their work. These

persons are called to join the congregation's nonstaff representatives in overseeing youth ministry.

The organizational structure and process presented here
places high value on both public (usually ordained) ministry
and the role of the congregation (the laity). Lay persons are
viewed as gifted Christians capable of taking responsibility for
the life and mission of their congregations. Professional lay
staff associates are considered important extensions of the ministry of the laity in some situations. Pastors are valued as persons trained and called to ministry; they are also charged with
supervisory tasks in the congregation. The organizational development, structure, and process presented is based on an
understanding of the church and its authority as presented in
Ephesians 4; it is also informed by the work of contemporary
organizational theorists who believe administration functions
best when lean and flexible, when structure and process serve
purpose and function, and when the integrity of every person
in the organization is honored. Structure and process are the
focus here. Persons in leadership will be discussed in the next
chapter.

Organizational structure

Four organizational spheres are necessary to focus and
channel a congregation's youth ministry. The first is the leader-
consultant team comprised of the congregation's youth ministry
representative and the pastor. In some congregations this team
will also include a staff associate with responsibilities in youth
ministry. The second sphere is the youth committee. The congregation's elected youth ministry representative is joined by
two to six other persons elected from the congregation to form
this committee. The pastor and youth ministry staff associate
are ex-officio members. The third sphere is the church council,
board of elders, or similar leadership group. This legislative-
judicial group formulates policy and coordinates the whole life
and mission of the congregation. The fourth sphere is the larg-
est. It is made up of all those who do hands-on ministry with
youth in the congregation and community.

Congregational youth ministry representative

The congregation's youth ministry representative (YMR) is in charge of youth ministry on behalf of the congregation. Between congregational and council or elders' meetings "the buck stops here." The YMR must be given power and responsibility; she or he must be held accountable. It's the YMR's responsibility to initiate conversation with the pastor about the nature of the congregation's ministry with youth. Together they design the processes and formulate the strategies for engaging the youth committee in shaping ministry with youth in the congregation. These persons need to meet frequently (at least once per month) to build trust and address the tasks at hand. The YMR is a member of the church council and chairperson of the youth committee. Deep faith, commitment to congregational ministry with youth, and administrative ability are the crucial attributes of a YMR. She or he is elected by the congregation to serve a three-year term. She can succeed herself once. The YMR chairs the youth committee as it makes decisions, gets the church council to ratify policies and strategies, and implements them in the congregation. The YMR takes initiative; he guides; he oversees; he is an advocate on behalf of the youth in the congregation and community. The YMR is the primary congregational leader in youth ministry.

Pastor

The pastor joins the YMR as a theological and ministerial consultant. The pastor brings expertise in theological inquiry and formulation. The pastor adds breadth gained from participation in the larger ministry of the church. The pastor is a resource, gadfly, and advocate. The pastor and YMR support each other in their work with the youth committee and the church council. If they disagree and cannot resolve their differences, they take them to the president of the congregation or, if necessary, to the church council.

Youth ministry staff associate

If a congregation has a youth ministry staff associate, that person joins the YMR and pastor in their deliberations. This person should bring theological and ministerial expertise. It's this person's responsibility to thoroughly know the youth and youth ministry activities of the congregation. This person should be trained and experienced in youth ministry. The youth ministry associate can supplement the pastor as a major staff person assisting the YMR in her work with the youth committee.

Youth committee

The youth committee of the congregation has legislative functions. It assists the YMR and the pastor in setting the congregation's direction for youth ministry. It identifies purpose and mission; it gathers and analyzes data about youth; it formulates policy and recommends such to the church council for approval; it designs broad strategies.

The youth committee's executive functions are advocating youth concerns, developing leadership, and overseeing youth ministry activities. It assists the YMR in making certain youth ministry is implemented. It does not do the hands-on work with youth, although one or more of its members may have particular gifts and responsibilities for such work.

Over half the persons on the youth committee are chosen by the congregation from among its junior highs, senior highs, and young adults. Its remaining members are adults chosen in the same manner. Its members serve staggered three-year terms. The youth committee vice president is in line to become the next YMR. The committee meets as often as necessary to build trust among its members and carry on its work. Usually this will be at least once per month.

Hands-on youth ministry

The hands-on work of youth ministry is accomplished by persons of particular gifts and a variety of responsibilities throughout the congregation. They may be persons who secure, train, and coordinate youth for assisting roles in worship; they may be the cadre of youth visitors who join the pastor or youth ministry associate in one-to-one ministry with youth; they may be the persons who oversee the internship program for confirmands or the one who leads clown ministry. This group of youth ministry leaders becomes as large as is needed to carry out the congregation's youth ministry activities.

These hands-on youth ministry persons are of all ages and have a variety of characteristics and capabilities. Most important among these characteristics are a lively faith and a commitment to youth ministry. These persons are identified and secured by the youth committee. The pastor or pastors must always be among those doing hands-on youth ministry. Some congregations will also have youth ministry staff associates carrying out aspects of this ministry with youth.

Long-range planning

Whenever else they meet, it is important that once per year as many persons as possible who are involved in all four spheres of youth ministry meet under the direction of the YMR and the pastor for a leadership retreat. The purpose of the retreat is inspiration, assessment, and planning for the future. If the scope of youth ministry is to be congregational, if there is to be genuine inclusion of youth in the mainstream of the church, and if youth are to have significant impact in the church's life and mission, then those who lead must share the vision and invest themselves in setting its direction.

How will a church do youth ministry? A congregation will do it together. The congregation's elected youth ministry representative and the pastor will take executive leadership. The youth committee will take legislative leadership and assist in selective executive functions. Persons throughout the varied life and mission of the congregation will do the hands-on youth ministry. Some congregations will be tiny and their spheres will contain few people; others will be huge and their spheres will include many persons.

Administration is absolutely necessary for congregational youth ministry. Where there is a church, it always exists in some form. The Spirit provides us with the wisdom and energy through the members of Christ's body to faithfully and effectively order life and mission with youth.

8

Leadership
for Youth Ministry

Effective youth ministry needs capable leaders who can assist Christian youth and adults in discovering and developing their own ministries among youth. Many people do not understand nor channel the faith which is within them. They need someone to assist them in celebrating faith's presence and discovering its unique powers for giving life to others.

Faith formation and ministry discovery are challenging, exhausting, and varied team tasks. They need to be done from the pulpit. Pastors must preach about baptism and the Spirit-endowed faith of youth. In order to do so, pastors need to know young people well enough to recognize faith's manifestations and articulately affirm its presence and power in language and images which capture these young people's imagination. Religious education activities (including confirmation programs) need to call forth faith awareness as they immerse youth in faith's experience and community. Religious education can move beyond instruction to faith-filled exploration, affirmation, and action throughout the adolescent journey to adulthood.

Persons leading the various ministries of the congregation must search among youth for those needed to carry on the church's life and mission. Pastors, parents, and congregational leaders can help youth consider a profession or life's work in the context of the Christian understanding of vocation. As young people face school and job decisions they can be assisted in making those decisions in the light of their Christian faith and their larger calling to ministry.

Young Christians in ministry

Every Christian young person is a minister. Baptism is both God's seal of salvation and commissioning for ministry. Even as the gospel of Jesus Christ creates new life, the Spirit empowers capacities for ministry in the church and the world. Young people minister through their personhood—their way of being and acting. Relationships with parents, siblings, and friends are ministries. School work, employment, and domestic responsibilities are occasions for serving others. Conversing with one's friends, caring for the earth, and volunteering at the suicide hotline minister to neighbor and world. Participation in the life of God's people and telling the story of faith foster the kingdom of God on earth. "You are a chosen people, a royal priesthood, a holy nation, a people belonging to God, that you may declare the praises of him who called you out of darkness into his wonderful light" (1 Peter 2:9).

A faith-formation and ministry-discovery process with inactive youth

Some Christian young people will not be attending church, listening to preachers, and participating in the life of the congregation. Studies tell us they will have left seeing little in the congregation of significance for them. For these young men and women, faith formation and ministry discovery must take a different tack. Such a discovery process could have several dimensions.

First, youth ministry leaders can go to youth where they live. Someone can go to their places—their homes, schools, concert halls, athletic fields, and cars. This means getting inside their symbols, meanings, and interests. It suggests listening to their conversations and observing their lives. Personal contact can be made. Relationships have to be built.

Second, someone can help them name or give language to their faith. When their faith appears, it can be recognized and affirmed. Sometimes it will take the form of confession of Jesus Christ as Lord. More often it will reveal itself as young people speak of their sources of life. Other times their faith will be revealed in their questions, hopes, and dreams. Persons are needed to delight in these faith manifestations and encourage their growth. In this process, the power of God's Word and the richness of the Christian faith are waiting to be mediated through the life of one who has won the right to be heard.

Third, someone needs to challenge young people. Questions can be asked. How do you experience what you believe? How do you best express it? Where does it lead? What capacities do you have to follow it through? How does God's love flow through you to give life to those around you? Perhaps this is the task of "wonderment." Is it not to join youth in celebrating their faith and muse about its leading?

Finally, someone can support youth. A life of faith is risky. Following one's faith can be lonely and dangerous. Sometimes it's confusing. Encouragement and friendship are needed to keep going. Partnership with another or others can make the difference between hope and despair. Perhaps at this point there might even be felt need for the community of faith with its worship and communion.

Adults in youth ministry

Like young people, adults have been baptized into ministry. These people have been endowed with Spirit-filled capacities and many are already at work with youth. These important youth ministers are often overlooked and not supported by congregations. Most notable among these are parents of adolescents and young adults, grandparents, adult siblings, public school teachers, coaches, law enforcement agents, and employers, as well as adult guarantors from the congregation. Not all of these adult roles are occasions for overt witness to the gospel of Jesus Christ. These people are, however, one source of life and faith to those youth whom they directly influence.

Many adult congregational members have direct, ongoing access to young people's lives. For some of these people, ministry with youth is given by blood lines or job responsibilities. Others love young people and are drawn to them. All of these adults have ministries with youth which can be explored and enhanced. For example, many grandparents possess great gifts for wise and loving relationships with their own or surrogate teenage grandchildren in the congregation. Skipping a generation eliminates much of the conflict in youth-adult relationships. Many young people speak of a grandparent as being the most significant adult in their lives. Usually the benefits of these relationships are mutual. Congregations can be catalysts in connecting, affirming, and supporting these and the ministries of other adults already ministering to youth.

Leadership in congregational ministry with youth

Congregations doing faithful and effective youth ministry are created by God through capable leaders. These leaders are the pastors, designated youth and adults, and in some situations, the youth ministry staff associates who form the leadership teams necessary for the task. They are crucial. Without them congregational youth ministry will cease to exist. If they are unfaithful and incompetent, youth ministry will be distorted, crippled, and anemic. Each brings their own knowledge and skill. Each has roles difficult, if not impossible, for others to perform.

Pastors in youth ministry

Pastors have a strategic place in youth ministry although they are not the youth ministry of the congregation, are not primarily responsible, and are not in charge of it. Nevertheless they have basic, powerful, designated responsibilities which are fundamental to strong congregational youth ministry. They can make lasting contributions to a congregation's ministry with youth, or they can become its greatest impediment.

Pastors must doggedly remain true to their call when ministering with youth. It is not easy. Many congregations attempt to keep them from doing so. Some congregations have the mistaken notion that youth ministry is primarily the pastor's responsibility and will consistently, overtly, and covertly pressure him or her to take charge of it or get him to do most of whatever they believe youth ministry to be. Most pastors have historically responded to this pressure either by agreeing to take charge or opting out and passing youth ministry on to someone else. Neither response is effective nor faithful to a pastor's call.

Every pastor's role has requirements mandating him to provide leadership in: (1) worship, (2) preaching, (3) visitation, (4) teaching, and (5) supervision. These are tasks for which a pastor has been educated and trained; these are tasks that are fundamental to faithful and effective youth ministry.

Pastors are the primary force in directing congregational worship. They bring theological understanding; they've been instructed in its planning; they're trained to carry out most of its tasks. Congregations give them great power and freedom in determining its scope and direction. Congregational worship is the central event in the life and mission of the congregation. It's the central event in youth ministry.

The pastor must see that worship belongs to the entire congregation, that it belongs also to young people. She or he must ask: Are youth involved up front in its leadership? Is their religious music reflected among the hymns? Are young people and their concerns reflected in the prayers? Do I know the young people and their concerns reflected in the prayers? Do I know the young people who are worshiping? Are their many gifts enriching our worship life? Are they directly involved in planning worship? A pastor needs to go beyond the questions to advocacy and implementation. A pastor will need help from designated youth and adults responsible for worship. She cannot do it all. Yet she must take initiative in providing a worshiping congregation where young people sense God is addressing them and they are responding with their own praise, prayer, and thanksgiving.

Proclamation of the gospel is as important to youth as it is to anyone else. If the pastor will not preach the good news so that youth can hear and understand, who will? Rock stars? Actors? Actresses? Coaches? Cult leaders? Are these the only voices we want them to hear?

Preaching to anyone is hard work. Preaching to young people is doubly difficult. There is usually an age and cultural barrier which pastors have a hard time bridging. It can be done. Pastors need to interpret young people and their cultures just as they need to interpret biblical texts. They can find forms of verbal expression that are true to the gospel and the preacher as well as communicate with youth. They can allow the texts to interpret, heal, and challenge youth.

In the life of an adolescent, the most significant symbol of God's gracious presence is a caring believer. There's probably no time in a human being's faith pilgrimage when personal contact from the church is more important. Among the significant symbol bearers of the Christian faith, pastors are some of the most skilled visitors. They have been trained to listen. Theirs is the art of pastoral conversation. They are called to guide, heal, reconcile, and sustain. Pastors have access to young people's lives. They can be there during crises; they can share celebrations. The full range of adolescent life pathos is theirs to tend. Teenagers need sensitive, genuine care. In order to be faithful and effective, pastors need to visit young people—not only because it is part of their call, not only because it is vital to young people's faith, but because pastors need to visit them in order to be effective worship leaders, pastoral preachers, and congregational administrators. Youth ministry is primarily ministry with persons; pastors are central figures in that personal ministry.

Pastors are teachers. The Christian faith has content. Faith is a relationship with a living God that calls for expression and reflection. Pastors have been instructed in Scripture and the faith traditions. They have been entrusted with faith's truth. Extensive, careful reflection and expression of faith's experience is at the center of their vocation. Pastors are specifically called to assist young people in learning Scripture and tradition and understanding life in light of their relationship with God. Pastors must lead their congregations in passing the Christian faith to each new generation. They join youth in the search for that which is good, right, and beautiful. Fostering Judeo-Christian values of freedom, love, and justice is one of their prime tasks. Pastors have responsibility for the formation of values upon which the future will be built. Pastors are congregational master teachers; they must teach youth well; they must assist others in teaching youth.

Pastors are called to supervise. They are to oversee, to carefully watch over. They are to manage, to tactfully order. They are to direct, to wisely guide. Pastors' theological development, training for ministry, and full-time participation in congregational life uniquely qualify them for joining the congregation's designated youth ministry representative in administering youth ministry.

Raising theological questions is one pastoral task in administrating youth ministry. Questions like: Where is Jesus Christ present and at work in young people's lives? What are we teaching youth about grace and stewardship? What does faith have to do with growing up? What do our understandings of gospel, church, and ministry teach us about youth ministry? These questions and their answers become the foundations and fountains from which youth ministries develop and flow.

Considering organizational structure and process is another pastoral ministry task. Pastors are to assist congregations in fashioning youth ministry which is faithful to the purposes of the gospel. They can use their vantage point and office to initiate and guide designated persons in the congregation to formulate direction, design strategy, select leadership, implement activity, and evaluate results. Without a pastor's advocacy, many congregations stay stuck in old ruts and stereotypes that inhibit youth ministry. Pastors have access to expertise and materials which they can broker to designated youth and adults carrying on the youth ministry of the congregation.

Worship, preaching, visitation, teaching, and supervision are pastoral roles in youth ministry. Even though pastors will not be the only ones in some of these roles, they have unique contributions in all. Some pastors will be more gifted in some dimensions than others. Some pastors in multistaff parishes will not be directly involved in each one. Every pastor must be trained to do something with them all. Seminaries are responsible to see that the foundations are laid. Together with other expressions of the church, seminaries must also see that these abilities have continued development and renewal.

Youth ministry staff associates

In most congregations, the pastor will be the only staff person working with youth. Some congregations will have more than one pastor with one or all of these pastors having extensive responsibilities for ministry with young people. Some congregations will call a lay person to full- or part-time youth ministry. These youth ministry staff associates are becoming more prevalent. Many church bodies now have procedures for certifying them. Institutes, colleges, and seminaries have developed programs to provide for their education.

Youth ministry staff associates can be great assets. In some congregations there are too many adolescents and young adults for one, or in some situations even two or more, of the pastors to visit and teach. In other situations there is too much effort needed to organizationally develop and oversee congregational youth ministry yet there is no need for another ordained person. Such situations are tailor-made for youth ministry staff associates.

Calling a youth ministry staff associate can be disastrous. They are often called because they are young, cheap, and available, not because they are competent. When pastors and congregations call youth ministry staff associates they tend to abdicate their responsibilities for ministry with youth, and "turn it all over to the one who's paid." They lose touch with young people. This can fragment and devalue ministry with youth in the church and community.

Youth ministry staff associates can be carefully chosen and wisely integrated into a congregation's ministry with youth. They can be chosen on the basis of personal characteristics and competence rather than age and economics. Lively faith, maturity, intelligence, integrity, commitment, openness, energy, confidence, and compassion are the crucial attributes. Biblical knowledge, theological understanding, administrative ability, and educational skills as well as visitation and counseling acumen are the key capacities.

Forging the youth ministry staff associate and the congregational youth ministry representative and the pastor into a central congregational youth ministry leadership team is of utmost importance. Working together, these people can harness the additional power of the youth ministry staff associate without negating the necessary roles of the YMR and pastor.

Continual care must be exercised so that even though the youth ministry staff associate becomes a central symbol in the congregation's youth ministry, he or she does not become the only symbol or the one doing most of the ministry. Even though a youth ministry staff associate will bring her own capacities for doing the hands-on work of ministry with youth, hers is primarily an administrative or facilitative role. Like a pastor or a congregational youth ministry representative, a youth ministry staff associate is there to help the congregation do its ministry with youth.

Designated youth and adults in youth ministry

Some from among the youth and adults of the congregation have particular gifts of leadership for focusing and expediting the congregation's ministry with youth. Among these will be administrators, visitors, teachers, musicians, journalists, photographers, artists, recreational experts, prophets, evangelists, cooks, backpackers, cyclists, dancers, actors, actresses, canoeists, worship leaders, or counselors—any youth or adult who has those peculiar skills which will facilitate the congregation's youth ministry.

Some of these youth and adults will be elected to leadership positions on the church council and committees. Youth and adults with special skills need to be appointed to lead congregational youth ministry efforts. Others will volunteer to serve. A few will take their own initiative for others to follow. Most must be carefully selected and trained; all must be supported in their work.

Youth ministry leadership discovery

Talent scouts are needed for this leadership discovery work. Somehow the gifts God gives the church through its youth and adults must be discovered and channeled. The congregation's youth ministry representative and the pastor are the congregation's primary talent scouts. They must be joined by the members of the youth committee. Every youth in the congregation can be considered. They can be surveyed, observed, or even interviewed. Some crucial gifts and abilities will be missing and will need to be developed. One might even keep records. A talent pool might be built. A "scouting book" on each youth could even be considered. Much the same could be done in the search for adults to work with youth in ministry.

Perhaps not everyone need be personally contacted, but no one should be left unconsidered.

What will the talent scouts look for in such youth and adult leaders? Of course the gifts peculiar to each task will vary. There are some characteristics one might agree would be common to all. These youth and adult leaders need to be persons with a curious, lively faith. They need to be knowledgeable. Independence and self-reliance are important. Relational and communicational capacities will be needed. They'll need to take some risks. They need to have confidence and be willing to learn.

The congregation's youth ministry representative, pastor, and youth committee can see that these youth and adults are made available to the leadership-determining processes of the congregation. Nominating committees for church offices, governing boards, and committees need to know of them. Committees that have responsibilities which affect youth in any way need to know of them. The youth committee which oversees those ministry activities with youth needs to know of their gifts.

Leadership training

Youth and adult leaders in the congregation's ministry with youth need to be educated, trained, and supported. Even though chosen because of their faith, knowledge, and skill, their work is difficult and unless they grow and find support, they will usually become frustrated and overwhelmed. They will all benefit by training which assists them with:

1. Faith formation—their own and its facilitation in others.
2. A vision of congregational ministry with youth.
3. Effective communication.
4. Group leadership and cooperative work skills.
5. Planning and problem solving.
6. Advocacy for youth.

7. Developing greater competence in their particular responsibility in youth ministry.

Facilitating growth in these areas is the responsibility of the YMR, the pastor, and the youth committee. They have a great many models at their disposal. Tutors or mentors can be tapped for learning many of these skills. Books and other literature provide help in others. Video and audio tapes can be found in several of these areas. Camp staffs can be tapped. Denominational offices and national youth agencies are excellent resources.

A leadership training model

There is an action-reflection leadership training model which effectively combines both training and support. In this model, all youth and adult leaders in ministry with youth usually meet four times per year—three times for four hours and once for a full day. Midfall, midwinter, and midspring they meet on an evening from 6 to 10 P.M. They begin with a sack supper. Then follows study of some aspect of youth ministry. Next, case studies from their work are considered in the light of the youth ministry study; possible new strategies are drawn. Then follows general discussion of the state and specifics of youth ministry in the congregation. The evening closes with a worship service which includes opportunity for supportive group prayer.

The full-day meeting during late summer follows much the same format except time is allowed for practice of that which has been taught. Some congregations and denominations stretch these events into five-day experiences in urban, wilderness, or rural settings; some hold them monthly throughout the school year. The purpose remains the same; it is to support and refine the abilities of leaders with the best of youth ministry theory and practice.

Who will do youth ministry? Youth in the congregation already are doing it. Many adults also are already engaged in youth ministry. Pastors have a specific role. Uniquely gifted youth and adults are needed to lead. Competent youth ministry staff associates bring special expertise to some churches. These persons become a broad-based team through which Christ continues ministry among his people and in the world.

9

Getting Youth Ministry Started

Reflection on God's gracious message was this book's beginning point. Life and mission, flowing from that message into the lives of young people, have been its focus. Youth ministry has been articulated within the framework of the New Testament view of ministry as worship, proclamation, education, communion, and service. Clues have been given to the direction and shape each of these might take. Many of the components and tasks in the development of congregational youth ministry have been introduced. Now they are woven into a process and presented as a full-blown portrait of ministry with youth in a congregation.

There is great risk in presenting a particular process and portrait of youth ministry. The portrait could be used to foist an unwanted, untailored youth ministry program on a congregation. A reader might view all that is portrayed and be overwhelmed. Someone could get caught up in the details and lose touch with the author's overall goal. Yet a portrait is present because there is greater risk in not doing so. Too often explorations of ministry only address the theoretical, leaving readers wondering about the theory's applicability. Some publications are smorgasbords of resources without unifying theological inquiry. This presentation of youth ministry is an attempt to move full circle. Therefore, the author ventures one portrait of youth ministry born of certain biblical and theological affirmations.

A word needs to be said about timing. Faithful and effective youth ministries are patiently grown, not mass-produced. The process and portrait of youth ministry presented assumes a congregation and pastor committed to deliberately and patiently creating quality youth ministry over time, perhaps even three to six years of time.

Taking a congregational and community youth ministry history

Developing faithful and effective youth ministry in a congregation begins by taking seriously that which already exists. The congregation's and community's past and present youth ministries are a part of the context within which one must work. There may be traditions which are sacred and will only mean resistance if ignored or directly violated. There may be old wounds and fears which must be addressed if there is to be growth. Every congregation has attitudes and expectations about young people and youth ministry. Each church and community has young people and adults of lively faith who are engaging somewhere, someway in faithful ministry with youth. These efforts must not be overlooked, hampered, or dismantled.

The congregation's youth ministry representative and the pastor need to seek out each other and develop a process for learning the history and assessing the present state of youth ministry in the congregation and community. Each person can take specific responsibilities for getting needed information quickly and simply.[1]

Focus on youth

Congregational youth ministry must be grounded in a clear understanding of the community's young people. Therefore, the next step might well be the congregation's youth ministry representative and pastor engaging the congregation's youth ministry leaders in discovering, tapping, and attending to young people's gifts and needs. These leaders might use a Community Field Study[2] and/or a Conversational Community Youth Inquiry which gets at youths' gifts and needs most quickly.[3]

Focus on message and mission

Next the pastor and the congregation's chief elected youth representative can engage the congregation's youth ministry leadership in a theological exploration of the message of the gospel and the life and mission of the church.[4]

A congregation might develop a youth ministry mission statement which contains a combination of theological foundations and key definitions based on its theological tradition. Much of my work is with Lutheran congregations, and an example of a statement I suggest for such churches follows:

Youth are called through Word and sacrament to full partnership in the community of faith and challenged to full participation in the life and mission of Christ's church. This means:
   1. Youth ministries are centered in Baptism, the proclamation and study of the Word, and participation in the Lord's Supper.
   2. Youth are the church of today as well as the church of the future.
   3. Youth ministries are ministries by, with, and for youth.
   4. Youth are to share in forming the church's theology and its resulting life and mission in the world.
   5. Youth ministries are integrated with and not separated from the mainstream of the church's life and mission.

Youth are members of the body of Christ who bring unique gifts and needs to the church. This means:
   1. Youth ministries are to discover and reflect the unique

gifts, needs, perspectives, issues, and energies of youth and their culture.

2. Youth ministries are designed to nurture the faith of young people within a life-long journey of learning.
3. Youth ministries are to provide youth-oriented relationships and events as well as involve youth in the wider life and mission of the church.
4. Youth ministries are to support and prepare youth and adults for their ministry with, by, and for youth.

Youth ministries attend to the full range of life issues of the youth of the congregation and the community. This means:

1. Youth ministries are person-oriented.
2. Youth ministries look beyond the youth group to the youth of the congregation and the community.
3. Youth ministries emphasize witness and service as well as nurture and community.
4. Youth ministries see all of life included in the reconciling gospel of our Lord Jesus Christ.

Youth are persons between the ages of 10 and 25.

Youth ministries are youth and adults working together so that youth might continue to grow and participate in their baptismal relationship to their Lord, others, themselves, and their world through the means of grace and the congregation's ministries of proclamation, teaching, worship, community, witness, and service.

The youth ministry mission statement which results from a theological exploration provides the congregation's youth ministry representative, pastor, and youth ministry leaders a lodestar by which to direct and shape ministry with youth. It articulates a preamble from which to present youth ministry to the entire congregation. It supplies a focus around which to stabilize and review youth ministry over the years. Without this intentional theological enterprise, youth ministry usually loses its way in a maze of activity or dies because it has wandered from its source of life.

Focus on organizational structure and process

The congregation's youth ministry representative and the pastor should next examine the existing congregational structures for carrying on youth ministry. They need to ask hard questions about the relationships between purpose and structure, power and accountability, as well as accessibility and flexibility. Do they provide youth ministry leaders direct access to the power center of the congregation? Are they designed to carry out the newly stated mission with youth? Are the structures clearly defined and accessible? If these questions do not have positive answers, a careful, deliberate reorganization can be undertaken with the help of the congregational president.

Many congregations don't have a position approximating a congregationally elected youth ministry representative. Some have one but do not have that person on the church council or board of elders. Some congregations have no youth committee; many do but do not have them considering the big questions of why and how rather than what. Working toward some such arrangement is strongly encouraged. Until there is a particular person whom the congregation has knowingly invested with the power and responsibilities of guiding youth ministry, until that person has direct access to the power structure of the congregation, thoroughgoing youth ministry efforts will be hampered and short-lived.

Changing the organizational structures and processes of a congregation can be very difficult. Inertia must be overcome. People have investments in leaving things the way they are. Changing a constitution or bylaws takes time and energy. If change is going to come constructively, the congregation must understand and own the need and direction of change. They need to be informed; they need to be listened to; they need to participate in determining whatever new structures and processes will emerge. Respectful, inclusive work on reorganization cannot only result in more effective ways of working but can also mean greater awareness of and support for youth ministry.

Effecting organizational change is an important ministry in the church. Usually someone in the congregation has the native abilities, training, and experience necessary for accomplishing this task. Any person who has the role approximating that of YMR can join the pastor in finding such persons and inviting their participation in the process.[5]

An organizational structure with four spheres of leadership persons is advocated by this author (see Chapter 7, p. 67). At the center, it provides a congregational elected youth ministry representative who sits on the church council, is supported by the pastor and carries the key responsibility for youth ministry leadership in the congregation. It provides a youth committee which formulates policy and assists in overseeing the congregation's youth ministry. It includes the church council or board of elders. It contains provision for a diverse team of people to do the hands-on work of youth ministry.

Starting or renewing youth ministry in a congregation is a delicate and difficult task. Respectful purposefulness is the key. Understanding a congregation's and community's youth ministry history is the place to start, understanding the gifts and needs of youth is another step, understanding the gospel and its implications for a congregation's mission and ministry with youth is still another, and designing an organizational structure fitted to that mission and ministry comes next.

These four preliminary steps create the solid center from which three types of youth ministries can meaningfully flow throughout the congregation and into the community. These three types of youth ministry activities focus in the congregation, among peers, and on individuals.

10

Congregational Youth Ministry Activities

Congregations in ministry with youth

Congregations do youth ministry. Wherever there are young people in a church or its surrounding community, a congregation does youth ministry. Some congregations do it well, others poorly. A congregation can be "youth friendly." It can be "youth indifferent." Some are straight-out "youth hostile." What makes the difference?

The gospel of Jesus Christ creates faith in those who hear and gather to receive God's continuing grace and truth. These people create a life together whose history, traditions, music, language, patterns, and dynamics reflect a variety of attitudes about youth. From these attitudes it is clear some churches believe youth are a rebellious threat to faith and must be firmly controlled. Others see them as immature and not ready for a significant life of faith. "Youth are to be seen and not heard," is the motto of many churches. Some churches are puzzled by young people and don't know what to do with them so they ignore them. A few are uneasy about them and would just as soon not have them around. Some churches decide what's best for youth, carry on without consulting them, and get angry at their recalcitrance when the young people do not respond. None of these are "youth friendly" congregations. Young people pick up these attitudes immediately. Their antennae are long and sensitive. They know when they are not welcome or valued, and they stay away or come under protest.

What is a "youth friendly" congregation? "Youth friendly" congregations have a conspicuous youth presence. In these churches youth are present in worship. They are seated in the pews. They are among those leading the service. They come to the church's informal gatherings. Some of them participate in the congregation's activities which are uniquely for youth.

"Youth friendly" congregations recognize and tap young people's power. They have youth on their central organizational councils and committees. They have them teaching the young, shaping thinking, visiting the aged, serving the poor, fighting oppression, and witnessing to the saving presence of God in their lives.

"Youth friendly" congregations value young people. They listen to them; they support them with prayer, time, facilities, and money. These congregations respond to the needs of youth. They develop specific programs with youth as well as integrating them into the congregation's ministry.

"Youth friendly" congregations are those where youth are present, powerful, and valuable in congregational life and mission.

Congregations can evaluate their "youth friendliness." The congregation's chief youth representative and the pastor might periodically engage a group of youth, the youth committee, and the church council in discussing these questions: Is our congregation a "youth friendly" place? Are youth present? Do they have power? Are they valued? Comparisons of the responses of the groups could be drawn. Issues would emerge and become focused. Decisions could be made and implemented. These would be some of the most important and

difficult moments in youth ministry and the life of the congregation.

There are often long-standing stereotypes and biases about
young people; these will not be changed easily. Every congregation has only so many resources; every group or vested interest has their argument for the priority of their concern. The
pastor and the congregation's elected youth ministry representative must be well prepared to present the case for the
importance of ministry with youth for the vitality of the church.
Here the theological arguments can be mounted; here the sta-
tistics and facts can be presented; here is one place for advocacy
and commitment. A congregation's leadership can decide to
rework its church into a "youth friendly" place.

Inclusive congregational worship

Worship is the single most important element of congregational youth ministry. If a congregation is to faithfully and
effectively join young people in their life with God, that congregation needs to develop its services into significant and
welcoming places for youth to worship.

In most congregations the pastor and music leaders determine the nature of worship. Some congregations have a
worship committee that guides its worship. Youth ministry
leaders need to tactfully raise these persons' awareness of the
importance of youth-inclusive worship.

The content of worship can be one focus of these aware-
ness-raising efforts. Various parts of the worship service and
other elements such as drama, banners, and worship themes
can reflect young people's life issues, responses to the gospel,
and need of healing. God's participation in young people's
personal, relational, and academic joys can be celebrated; their
faith questions need to be addressed; individual family and
peer struggles call for attention; their hectic lives need interpretation. The Lord of the earth, the Christ of the church, and
the Jesus of their personal experience can be the focus of the
services.

The form of worship can be another focus. Language, symbols, music, dance, and ritual are born in the consciousness of persons in a particular culture. Young people share many of these art forms with adults; youth possess others which are uniquely their own. Every congregational worship service might well include one child's song or religious folk hymn which is familiar to young people. Organs and pianos need to be supplemented with violin, brass, drums, and guitar. Youth are masters at capturing enthusiasm in short phrases and banners. Their artwork is often bold, straightforward, and profound. There are full worship formats such as the Chicago Folk Mass which young people find particularly appropriate. The media's influence on youth must be taken seriously. Puppetry, clowning, mime, drama, and liturgical dance are effective modes of communication with persons of an electronic consciousness. Youth's intolerance of boredom can be an early sensor of a worship service's deadening influence on all in attendance; young people's need for crisp movement and variety can press worship leaders to involve everyone in more lively worship.

The leadership of worship can be yet another focus. Worship leaders are symbols of faith. They focus one's relationship with God, each other, and the world. Women, the young, and the old are needed in liturgical leadership if worship is going to become more inclusive. Young people can move beyond such basic roles as lighting candles. They are capable of ushering, reading Scripture, leading prayers, singing, and playing instruments. They often are the most active musicians in the congregation. Some already play in musical groups. Many can join adults in forming brass ensembles, string quartets, or flute duets. Youth choirs can start with a duet or a trio which becomes a larger group. Some young people are creative photographers and fine artists capable of turning a nook, a wall, a chancel, or the beams of a sanctuary into placards of the gospel.

Pastoral preaching

Good preaching is crucial to youth ministry. Young people have even lower tolerances than adults for superficial and dull sermons. Good preaching may not bring them, but poor preaching turns them away from worship and creates a barrier between them and the institutional church. Young people have need for liberation, forgiveness, reconciliation, and hope. Like adults, they respond to words that capture their imaginations, interpret their worlds, and lift their spirits.

Most of the elements that make for good preaching to adults make for effective communication of the gospel to young people. Their preachers need to know the biblical story and understand the issues at stake in the scripture texts. Their sermons need to wrestle with substantive life concerns in clear, crisp language. Youth want the message to mean something to its presenter. Youth find the grace of God in lively prose, parable, and poetry. They yearn for interesting sermons which say something significant about that which matters. Young people discover grace in the comical and the humorous. The preacher needs to make contact with their minds, emotions, and wills. She or he has about 20 minutes to do so.

Even though most of their life and death issues are similar to those of their parents, youth have their own stage and backdrops upon which this drama is worked out. Preachers need to take these stages and backdrops with utter seriousness. Those who would preach to youth will need to get onto young people's stages and into their world. The consciousness of youth is different than that of most adults. They've grown up in a barrage of stimulation. They are accustomed to intense, multileveled communication. Analytical, propositional, verbal symbols are not going to get through to them. Theirs is largely a right brain world which thrives on story, parable, and fantasy. They need sermons with concrete images spoken in words of their everyday conversation. This does not mean using their jargon; it means knowing their jargon; it means preaching clearly, simply, and specifically.

Pastors can learn to preach to young people. In the process they may improve their ability to communicate with all age groups. Preachers can have significant contact with youth, their language, and their world. Observing them at school, in the community, and at church will be helpful. Preachers can engage youth in conversation over breakfast or lunch and listen, listen some more, and then listen again. Those who would preach to young people might well read their magazines, periodically studying *Seventeen, Sports Illustrated, Rolling Stone* or some of the new interest tabloids. Going to the movies they frequent or tuning in to their favorite television shows provides other entrees to their consciousness. Preachers can read the authors who communicate with young people. They can learn from the comedians who command their attention. They might listen to the singers who create their music. Every pastor might gather around him a handpicked group of articulate adolescents and young adults who become partners in preaching through periodic consultation on texts and sermons.

Lifelong learning

A lifelong learning perspective suggests youth leaders join those working with children and adults in asking: What's happening with Christians in the spring, summer, fall, and winter of their faith life? What questions are being asked when? What gifts do persons of each age bring? How do persons in these seasons instruct and nurture one another? How do we best join their pilgrimage in each season? Youth ministry is a cooperative enterprise in the intricate web of a congregation's life and mission with people throughout their lives.

Confirmation

Some Christian churches have a confirmation tradition with enough force to involve their adolescents in educational ministry. This tradition provides Christian congregations with access to young people's faith at a crucial but difficult point in their development. Congregations face the challenge of engaging this captive audience in significant growth. Failure to do so has the potential of souring these young people's view of the church and stunting their faith. For those congregations who do not have confirmation in their traditions, the following concepts will apply to their educational ministries with youth.

Understood in the context of lifelong learning, confirmation can afford to be less ambitious. It does not have to impart the whole counsel of God. It is not the final indoctrination in adult faith. Understood in the context of adolescent uniqueness, confirmation can be more focused. It can engage young persons in learning commensurate with their development. It can use learning experiences tailored to their consciousness. Understood in the context of congregational life and mission, confirmation can be more integrated. It can be anchored in community. It can interface young people with the larger life and mission of the congregation.

Most adolescents participate in confirmation because they must. Confirmation classes are captive audiences. What does the gospel do with captives? What will the gospel do with this captive audience? Wrestling with this question is one of the fundamental tasks in creating a faithful and effective confirmation ministry. The gospel frees. Confirmation can free. Someplace very early in confirmation, each confirmand needs to be surprised by grace. Each confirmand can be genuinely accepted and affirmed. Meeting them in their faith struggles with the appropriate expression of love and truth frees them. Creating an inquisitive and fun-loving learning community provides motivation and supportive friendships. Significant challenges and accomplishments enhance self-worth and meaning. Confirmation ministry needs to transform an attitude.

Faith formation is multidimensional and must be reflected in the goals, content, and approaches of confirmation. Faith has content; there is a message. Faith has emotion; there is pathos and inspiration. Faith creates community; it involves one in relationships. Faith cares; there are decisions and values.

Faith has power; it acts, heals, sustains. During confirmation, an entire person of faith is being formed in his or her life with God in the midst of the world.

No single confirmation ministry will fit every congregation. No church can expect to simply order a ready-made confirmation ministry from denominational headquarters, a publisher's catalog, or the next congregation. Each of these can provide excellent resources. However, confirmation ministry needs to be custom-designed. Every congregation needs one person on the youth committee in charge of confirmation ministry. Joined by the pastor and someone from the congregation's education committee, this person needs to guide a congregation in designing and implementing a confirmation ministry that fits the congregational and community situation.

Confirmation ministry can have high congregational priority and few but specific expectations. In many congregations it's just the opposite. Congregations need to be realistic and clear about their expectations. They can identify those areas in which they want confirmands to have examined and affirmed their faith. Congregations need to draw on their most capable educators, provide their pastors quality time and supply ample funds. They should not place the entire responsibility on their pastor. It's important for them to courageously look at the effectiveness of their programs.

Pastors need to be faithfully and effectively involved in some aspect of confirmation ministry. Many pastors loathe teaching confirmation. A majority of pastors say they do not know how to teach teenagers. Congregational youth ministry leaders and pastors can deal with these attitudes and poor teaching skills. Most pastors can be trained to be effective teachers of small groups of teenagers. Most communities have at least one effective junior high teacher who can be a pastor's tutor. There are continuing education workshops available where pastors can learn pedagogy appropriate to adolescents. A few pastors will never be able to teach young people. If so, they need to become theological consultants to those who can do it well.

Some pastors who are poor teachers are excellent listeners. These pastors might spend quality time getting to know each confirmand. A congregation with such a pastor might use individualized confirmation instruction for a large part of its ministry. If pastors loathe confirmation ministry and are doing it ineptly, the pastor and his attitude become the unfortunate primary message.

Confirmation ministry is best accomplished in clearly identified, readily accomplished, short segments over a long period of time. Confirmation ministry constructed as one, two, or three years of weekly classes over the school year will always be an uphill battle. Confirmation becomes a marathon; the goal is to get through. Some segments might well be accomplished on one- or two-day retreats. Those meeting weekly can be six- to eight-week series with breaks for Advent and Lent when pastors and students are especially busy. Perhaps a segment might be designed as a five-day summer camp experience between eighth and ninth grades. One module could be a three-day experiential learning experience in the city or the wilderness. Another might be an individual research and writing project completed over four to six weeks before being confirmed. Eight- to 10-week Sunday school quarters might be used for a film series on the Old or New Testament or for reading and discussing *The Chronicles of Narnia*.[1] These segments need to be developed with consistency, coherence, and momentum so that they carry the learning process from one stage to the next.

Parents need to be involved in confirmation. Confirmation curricula can be vehicles through which young people and parents engage in mutual faith inquiry. Youth can learn from what their parents believe. Confirmation curriculum can be used which requests confirmands to ask specific faith questions of parents. The adult educational ministry of the congregation can prepare confirmation parents for their teenagers' questions. Specific segments of confirmation can involve a parent or parents in mutual learning experiences with their confirmand.

Study of the First Article of The Apostles' Creed could include parental participation with confirmands in learning about familial influences on self-worth, anorexia, and chemical dependency. Study of the Fourth Commandment can include parental and confirmand exploration not only of the dynamics of the promise within the commandment but the multigenerational system in which the "honoring" of father and mother is accomplished. Parents can join their confirmands in studying teenage suicide and human sexuality in conjunction with the Fifth and Sixth Commandments. The Ninth and Tenth Commandments might provide the occasions for family financial values to be clarified and examined in the light of the Christian faith.

Parents and their confirmands can be visited together in their homes by the pastor or youth ministry leader who gets to know them, listens to their concerns, and interprets the church's confirmation ministry. Rather than demand that parents support the church in its confirmation ministry with their teenager, youth ministry leaders can design vehicles through which parents channel their concern and support.

Confirmation ministry might well include an internship in congregational leadership. Each confirmand can be assisted in discovering the gifts the Holy Spirit has given her or him for ministry in Christ's body. These gifts become the basis for a choice of congregational ministry in which the confirmand would serve during the later year of her confirmation experience. Every young person would be assigned an adult mentor in their area of the church's ministry. The confirmand can serve alongside her mentor who would teach her ministry, become acquainted with the student, and share with her the mentor's faith and life in the church. Confirmation ministry needs to be more than reading, seeing, and receiving. A person remembers little of what she reads; she remembers most of what she does.

Confirmation ministry must not be merely an individualized experience. Faith is corporate. To believe in Jesus Christ is to belong to his body. Confirmation ministry needs to foster community. It needs to be participation in communion. Forgiveness, reconciliation, and love can become more than words. Confirmation ministry needs to foster mutual conversation and caring. It can do so between individuals, within small groups, throughout the youth community, among the entire congregation. Experiential education, cooperative projects, "new games" recreation, small group discussion, internships, and retreats are ready resources for community building. Used wisely, they can add momentum to a confirmation ministry that understands itself as a vehicle for young men and women to more deeply experience the life of the church.

Confirmation ministry needs to be couched in ritual, gifts, and celebration. All along the adolescent faith journey, growth can be honored and encouraged. After a one-day Saturday retreat with their parents, students could well celebrate their first communion at a festive Sunday worship service. A banquet for them and their families served by the congregation could follow. At this banquet, they might even be given a personal copy of the church's hymnal. At the beginning of their systematic review of the biblical message, one could give them a sturdy study Bible. *The Chronicles of Narnia* might well be given each confirmand before they discuss them in Sunday school. The confirmands and their mentors could be commissioned at a worship service at the beginning of the student's last year in confirmation. They could be interviewed by the members of the church council to determine their readiness to reaffirm their faith as an adult. The rite of confirmation can be a festive worship service where pastors, parents, and faith mentors participate in the laying on of hands. No two congregations will celebrate this faith journey the same way. Each church will find its own way to express its support, recognition, and expectations of its newly emerging adults of faith.

Congregational community

Young people spend most of their time with their peers. Schools, sports, and leisure activities separate them from children and adults. Congregational life offers an opportunity to integrate young people with persons of all ages.

Youth ministry leaders can invite others in the congregation to join them in creating a few all-congregational events and rituals. An annual congregational weekend retreat might be deliberately designed for congregational integration. Monthly Sunday luncheons sponsored by single young adults could be open to the entire congregation. Some congregations may sponsor a regular schedule of congregational meals followed by the Lord's Supper. The congregation's annual meeting might include a ministry recognition banquet. Each congregation can find its own way to celebrate its life together.

Integration of youth in the congregation does not always happen. Youth ministry programs can fragment congregations. Youth leaders need to pay attention to the effect of their ministry on family and congregational life. Separate youth ministry activities can be held to a minimum. Ways and means for youth ministry with children and adults need to be promoted. Single-generation events can include intergenerational elements. Transgenerational and intergenerational events need to be planned. Young people have great gifts to give the aged and vice versa. Young people need small- and large-group mutual experiences with persons the age of their parents. In many communities all three generations rarely have an opportunity to share life with one another.

Vocation

Christians believe Jesus Christ transforms their relationship to all of life. Christians stand in a new relationship with God, people, and the earth. In their Baptism young people have been commissioned stewards of the planet, witnesses of Jesus Christ, and caretakers of those who need a physician.

Personhood, friendship, marriage, parenthood, church membership, employment, and citizenship become expressions of young people's faith. A Christian's vocation is his or her entire life-response to the gospel.

Youth ministry leaders can communicate this vision to young people. They can assist youth in working out the vision in their approach to life. They can provide handles for harnessing youths' spirit-endowed gifts.

Youth ministry might well assist young people to be faithful stewards of their primary relationships, church membership, work, and citizenship. Perspectives, processes, and possibilities can be provided for serving God and humankind in each of these areas.

Youth and family ministry

Families are young people's primary relational vocations. Youth are called by God to minister to their parents, step-parents, siblings, grandparents, and other relatives. These people need physical, emotional, relational, intellectual, and spiritual support from adolescents and young adults. Divorcing, single-parent, and blended families provide new challenges for teenagers. Youth forums, workshops, study-action groups, and retreats are good settings in which to teach young people knowledge and skills for their relational ministries.

At many levels, youth ministry is family ministry. Family is an important source of security and stability for youth. Renegotiating family relationships, beliefs, and values is an important part of the adolescent journey. The best indicator of whether or not teenagers will be active worshipers and congregational participants is the past and continuing participation of their parents in the life of the church. Following young people in their personal struggles almost always leads at some point to difficulties in their families. Whatever else youth ministry is, it is ministry to their parents and families.

Youth ministry leaders may want to provide some inter-generational and family learning settings. Parents and siblings

can join young people in developing healthy ways to care for
each other. Each of these offerings might well challenge young
people not only to take responsibility for themselves, but also
to look at their responsibilities to other persons in the family.
Teenagers are not wholly responsible for their families; neither
are their parents. Both need to work to make families healthy
places to live.

Occasions, processes, and resources for identifying and
supporting the ministries of parents and families abound. One
could begin with a class on faith formation in the family for
parents of children about to be baptized. John Westerhof III's
book, *Bringing Up Your Children in the Christian Faith*,[2] would
be one excellent text. A congregation might involve parents
directly in a child's faith formation from birth through young
adulthood by providing literature and media for them to use
with their children for instruction and discussion. Arch Books
Series,[3] *The Bible: Its Story for Children*,[4] *The Way of the
Wolf*,[5] *The Return of the Wolf*,[6] *The Chronicles of Narnia*,[7] and
Hind's Feet on High Places[8] are just a few of the excellent
resources available. The church can be a vehicle for strength-
ening marriages during the early, difficult, and crucial parenting years. Marriage enrichment models are numerous.[9]
Good materials are available for assisting both single- and dual-
parent families with parenting.[10] During these early family life
activities much of the groundwork for parenting teenagers can
be laid through these years of building relationships and faith
patterns.

During the adolescent years of the children, parents can
be supported in their ministries through carefully tailored participation in first communion, confirmation, or preparation for
Baptism.

Many Christian churches instruct children before they receive their first communion. If parents are included in this
process, they can be refreshed in their understandings of communion and prepared for conversations with their children
about forgiveness and reconciliation. This instruction can move

beyond theory to experientially exploring forgiveness and reconciliation between the parents, between parents and their children, as well as between them and God. Questions like "What shape will continuing community with God and each other take now that the child is becoming an adult?" need to be explored. Parents can speak of their experience of communion as one aspect of their children's exploration of its meaning. All this adds up to significant parent/child communication about faith. Preparation for and celebration of first communion can be events within which parents and their children integrate faith and life through vehicles provided by the church.

Parents of beginning confirmands can be provided information on adolescence. Merton and Irene Strommen's *Five Cries of Parents,*[11] *How to Live Almost Happily With Your Teenager* by Lois and Joel Davitz,[12] or the Center for Early Adolescence's *For Parents of Early Adolescents*[13] are excellent resources. More importantly these parents can be invited or requested to participate in a four- to six-week Sunday morning adult education class where these resources and presentations on parenting adolescents are discussed.

Many parents focus so strongly on nurturing and taking responsibility for their children that they have difficulty getting their children to grow up and leave them. In a technocratic society with its extended period of dependence, many young adults and parents have difficulty either living together or leaving each other. They get stuck. Parenting classes can help dads and moms prepare their children for self-reliance and interdependence. Family classes grounded in family system theory can help families look at their dynamics and participate in developing emotional, economic, physical, relational, and spiritual maturity. Young adult classes can help them individuate and mature, take responsibility for themselves, and proceed with their "vocation" as friend, neighbor, worker, and citizen.

Gifts of the Spirit

Youth have a right to full participation in Christ's church; they also have a responsibility to participate fully in its life and mission. Youth as well as adults can be introduced to the biblical understandings of stewardship. Within this larger stewardship perspective, youth ministry leaders might well guide young people in discerning their Spirit-given abilities for building up the body of Christ. Every young person can identify their particular gifts and offer them in the life and mission of the congregation. Every Christian youth has them; unless their congregation has tapped these ministry gifts, Christ's body remains crippled in that time and place.

Work

What will I do when I grow up? This fundamental vocational question is asked by nearly every youth. It's behind the question of whether or not to go to college. It's a factor in which vocational school or college to attend. It's often the source of great confusion and frustration. It's a felt need of youth which the church might well address in the context of Christian vocation.

Youth ministry leaders could sponsor a series of youth forums in the fall of each year (or every other year in a very small congregation) in which high school juniors and seniors were personally invited to a four- to six-week series on faith and work. Biblical and confessional understandings can be tapped to introduce work as ministry. The Strong-Campbell Vocational Test[14] might even be administered. Adult members of the congregation could be invited to speak about their work as an expression of their faith. Over a long weekend or Christmas vacation, a travel trip might be planned to representative vocational, state, private, and parochial schools. Most often young people are encouraged to look at career planning in the light of their own interests; youth ministries can help youth expand that view to include the good of their world and service to their God.

Citizenship

Life is a public matter. So is faith. Christians serve God through their public life. Youth ministry leaders and young people need to look with eyes of faith at their life within the institutions of the community, state, nation, and world. Each can challenge the other to consider elections, public debate, legislative processes, and community service as arenas for supporting a way of life commensurate with the convictions inherent in one's faith. Young adult forums might invite or discuss candidates at election time. Study-action groups might well consider public issues particularly germane to young people. Letters need to be drafted, debated, and sent to the editor. Community projects and candidates will need volunteers. Respect for property often requires consciousness-raising. Someone will be needed to write faith-informed statements on issues. Each young person will have his own way of participation. Congregational youth ministries need to lead both young people and adults to see citizenship as an arena in which to serve their Lord.

Finance

Faithful and effective youth ministry are costly. It requires serious thought, careful planning, quality time, competence, and money. The amount of money required to carry on youth ministry will vary from congregation to congregation. The way money is gathered and spent will be as significant as the amount available.

In most congregations, adult and childhood ministries are largely funded from the churches' budgets, yet young people must raise money for their ministries. There is some good reasoning in this. Adults give greater amounts of money; consequently, they have the right to decide its use and to be recipients of its ministry. Children must be taken care of by their parents. Young people don't give much. They have some abilities to earn money. Consequently, they can work to fund their own ministries. But there is some devastating theological impact in this. Young people learn that in the Christian faith, as most everywhere else, money equals power; those who can afford ministry get it. In this concept of youth ministry funding, they also are not assisted in becoming stewards of their considerable discretionary income. In both cases their views of grace and life are distorted.

Every adolescent and young adult can be taught and immersed in a biblical and theological attitude toward money and offerings. Young people have great amounts of discretionary income. Adolescents and young adults can be introduced to the joy of giving. Youth ministry leaders can assist teenagers in expressing their gratitude to God through: (1) giving from the top of their income, (2) giving a percentage of their income (the Scriptures suggest 10 percent as a guideline), or (3) giving sacrificially in response to human need. Approaches can be developed to introduce these stewardship notions to youth. Young people can serve God through substantial financial offerings.

As they are encouraged and expected to financially support their church's ministry, their ministries should be substantially supported by their church's budget. Facilities, leadership training, transportation, ministry resources, and outreach most often have price tags. Youth ministry leaders need to enumerate these costs as they strategize for ministry and make their requests clearly and compellingly known to the congregation's budget committee.

Fund raising certainly has a place in youth ministry. Fundraising events can be effective community-building experiences. Here youth and adults working side by side learn to know each other, support each other, and create a community spirit. Fund raisers can generate awareness, enthusiasm, and monies for fighting injustice and caring for the broken. Fund raising can enable youth to afford experiences in faith formation which would be available no other way. Many congregations creatively design these fund-raising experiences so that hours put in are translated into income credit toward a particular youth ministry event. Congregations will develop their own style of financing youth ministry. There need to be theological, moral, and contextual considerations in their choice of methods. The offerings and fund-raising approaches should be balanced in their style. The amount of money spent, the way the money is gathered, and the way it is used are all critical indicators of a congregation's understandings of the gospel.

Congregational youth ministry activities emphasize young people's common life with others in the church. Even though these activities are foundational, young people need different kinds. Some of their ministry is best accomplished with their peers. We turn there next.

11

Peer
Youth Ministry Activities

Worship with youth

Young people have life rhythms and sensibilities that call for worship experiences uniquely their own. Confirmation groups who share a common faith journey need to worship regularly. Small Bible study and growth groups have discovered worship grows out of their life together. Older high school and college students find midweek, late-evening communion services refreshing. Services of prayer, support, and healing are particularly meaningful around a friend's accident, illness, or injury. Moves, graduations, and deaths push young people to the limits and move them toward God and one another. Worship services at youth gatherings, retreats, and camps have had great impact on thousands of young people.

Music ministry

Music is a major dimension in young people's worship experience. Songs, instruments, and singing move them.

Every congregation needs musical leadership in youth ministry. At least one person who can sing, play an instrument, and lead singing needs to be planning and doing hands-on youth ministry in a congregation. Hopefully there will be several youth and adults doing so. A congregation's youth committee needs to scour the congregation and community until they find such musical leadership. The congregation's high school and college students are potential sources of candidates. Church musicians, church music leaders, pastors, school and community music leaders can be helpful consultants and perhaps even available to provide the leadership. Once identified, this person in musical leadership can be supplied training, money for musical literature, and support.

A high school or college age music leader in a congregation can develop a collection of the finest folk songbooks and liturgical resources available. The best songs from among these can be printed on poster board and taught youth whenever the occasion presents itself. A list of the congregational youths' favorite singable songs needs to be prepared, continually updated, and made available to those planning regular worship. In congregations of sufficient numbers of youth, this person might be invited to give leadership to an annual musical to be presented to the congregation and community.

Clowning, mime, puppetry, liturgical dance, and drama are effective media for youth ministry worship. They allow a young person to get involved in worship leadership without being the direct focus of public attention. They encourage and free the playful, creative side of participants. Preparing for these involves youth in exploring the meaning of Scripture and faith. Each of these vehicles of expression cultivates the imagination of the worshiper. One person in the congregation can be identified and trained to develop different media for use throughout the youth ministry of the church. A list and repertoire of effective skits can be made available. A group of youth could be encouraged to create a cast of puppet characters who do short presentations of scripture stories and parables. Many college and university campus ministries have clown troupes who will help congregations start one among their high school students and young adults.

Young people need times of solitude and renewal. "Remember the Sabbath day by keeping it holy" is an invitation to restoration. These Sabbaths may not all come a week at a time. They can take the forms of yearly or quarterly renewal events, designed to take young people into a different time frame, setting, and focus. Youth yearn for "mountaintop" experiences; they need days alone in the "wilderness." Some retreat or camp communities provide these time frames, settings, and foci. Nature can provide many others. Church sanctuaries on open countrysides, mountains, and beaches can be inexpensive places for shifting gears to reflection, journaling, conversation, prayer, and rest. Although young people initially resist the notion, most find it possible and profitable to "be still and know that I am God."

Placarding the saints and the prophets

Every generation has outstanding men and women whose words and deeds communicate the message of the gospel with sparkling clarity. Their speech and activities make them uniquely qualified to bear witness to young people. Youth seek models who provide possible patterns for their lives.

These individuals exist in almost every time and place. They can be found in every congregation and community. They are present among young people themselves. Some are well-known; others are inconspicuous. Youth ministry leaders can watch and search for them. Usually saints and prophets bear witness most effectively if someone interviews them with young people present and ready to ask questions. Some of these people live elsewhere on the planet. Television vignettes, newspaper clippings, and magazine articles can be edited into videotape, slide, and oral presentations of their words and deeds. Some of them have become the subjects of television and film documentaries. Many are directly available for interview through inexpensive speaker phones. Some of these persons are outstanding speakers. Youth ministry leaders can invite these spokespersons to community, conference, or national youth events; they can get them videotaped and available to small groups.

Bill was 19, handsome, paraplegic, and an alcoholic. He spoke slowly and directly of his life in a wealthy family. He was already a heavy pot and alcohol user the day he turned 16 and got his driver's license and a Corvette.

One rainy Friday evening during his senior year, following a party in which he had been drinking heavily, he challenged a friend to a drag race. Minutes later, he lost control of his car at 90 miles per hour òn a wet curve and severed his spinal cord.

His pot-smoking, drinking, and playboy life-style didn't end with his accident. During the days following his recovery from the accident, he used the chemicals and trips to the Bahamas and Las Vegas as salve for his pain. He was often angry, sometimes arrogant, mostly desperate.

One night in the depths of his depression he called a hotline, and after six months of playing cat and mouse with sobriety, he entered treatment for chemical dependency.

Bill told the students of this continuing struggle with his disability; he wondered if he could ever accept it. The confirmation class seated around his wheelchair sat in rapt attention as he spoke of his faith in God and his participation in the supportive relationships of Alcoholics Anonymous as his foundations for a new life. Long after the confirmation session was over, the students were still asking his views on the drinking age and the use of marijuana. He became a confidant for many younger youth at the church. He was a significant symbol of faith and life.

Testifying on the issues

Youth ministry leaders can gather young people for study, discussion, and formulation of faith-informed responses to the tough issues in adolescent and young adult lives. The results of these efforts might well appear in church bulletins and newspaper editorials as a part of the testimony of young women and men of faith. Some statements may be longer and get printed as pamphlets or position papers. Some of the testimony may lead to personal, social, or political action. It's vitally important that young people speak their convictions in the process. Experts among the faithful need to be invited to contribute. Unanimity on answers is not necessary; faithful grappling with that which matters and effective speaking with those who struggle is the goal.

The life issues which call for consideration will vary with time and place. Several areas of young people's lives frequently take center stage. Drinking laws, teenage pregnancy, abortion, public school policies, minimum wage laws, divorce, blended families, living together without being married, suicide, chemical abuse, rock music, and anorexia provide possibilities from which most youth leaders might choose one or two to get started.

If the proclamation of the church is to be credible to young people, its faith needs to make a contribution to the battle for youths' minds and well-being.

Other proclaimers

The church is not alone in having a message to proclaim in today's world. Many voices can be heard. Some of these voices are those of Christians working outside the mainstream of the church. Others may not profess Jesus Christ as Lord, but their message may be worth hearing and reflecting on.

Films and television specials are among the most powerful of these sources of proclamation. Modern technology has made these media presentations inexpensively and readily accessible for use in ministry. Nearly every congregation has someone who has a video player. Youth ministry leaders can be alert to the multitude of materials available and can design formats for their viewing and discussion.

Crucibles for faith formation

Adolescents and young adults have few arenas in which to articulate, explore, and formulate the questions, assumptions, and affirmations of their faith. Their lives are constantly barraged with information, much of which seeks to win their minds to a particular view of life and its ultimates. Youth develop the ability to filter out much of it. Yet, they need friendly places in which to examine what they've been taught in the light of their own convictions.

Focused conversation provides the occasion for this faith formation. Youth ministries can promote one-on-one dialog and small group discussions guided by skilled leaders. Youth ministry leaders can deliberately develop visitation ministries in which the pastor and other trained youth and adults are responsible for regular contact with youth. Such contacts can deliberately stimulate serious conversation about life and faith.

Weekly sack suppers, backpacking trips, bike treks, experiential education modules, and retreats are all potential occasions for small group discussions. The formats for these discussions and dialogs will vary with persons and settings. They might well include: (1) focus on an area of life such as friendship or values or vocation, (2) description of the youth's present experience in that area, (3) expression of questions, feelings, and convictions, (4) exploration of alternative points of view, including those within the Christian faith, (5) formulation or reformulation of one's point of view, and (6) drawing implications for new attitudes and actions.

The dialogs and discussions need to be led by skilled listeners with accepting attitudes who are able to follow young people in their thinking and speaking. Youth ministry can launch young people into lives lived more directly from their faith convictions.

Bible study

The Scriptures have been a source of liberation, instruction, and inspiration for Christians of all ages since the formation of the canon. Their mysteries never seem to be fully understood even by those who have given their lives to biblical interpretation. Yet, the Scriptures speak clearly to human concerns. They speak to the faith and life of adolescents and young adults.

Youth leaders can design educational ministries that guide young people into the Bible. These ministries cannot be lectures on Scripture. Those who lead them must be knowledgeable but able to join youth in mutual exploration of the biblical message. Small groups of young people, committed to study over a designated period of time, usually are effective vehicles. Each participant needs a Bible written in clear English. The leader should have a brief, lay Bible commentary at hand. Only a few verses should be considered at a time. These verses need to be seen in their context as part of a section or book or series of books and finally as a part of the full message of Scripture.

There is an old Bible study method which guides participants in asking four questions of the biblical text: (1) What do the words and sentences actually say? (2) What is the message of these verses? (3) What do these verses mean to me? (4) What are these verses suggesting about who I am and what I do? Lyman Coleman's Serendipity Series[1] has several excellent formats for experiential Bible study. Dennis Benson's Bible studies[2] afford young people another interesting approach to the text. The Scriptures are most helpful when studied in the context of life's everyday questions, the mutual conversation and consolation of Christians, and prayer.

Youth forums

Young people consistently face complex decisions and issues. Youth ministry leaders can provide them invaluable assistance and support as youth make choices. Within the perspectives of the Christian faith and the context of the Christian community, youth ministry leaders and youth can explore these issues, search for informed resources, consider alternatives, and formulate responses. Chemical use, sexual values, family conflict, vocational choices, economic pressures, and peer relationships are significant issues for most adolescents and young adults. Young people in each congregation and community will have their own issues.

Youth forums designed to explore these issues need to be well conceived and led. They might be guided by a youth/ adult team. The leaders need to be skilled in group process. They need to provide rhythms of reflection, presentation, conversation, discussion, and formulation. Quality resources abound: informed persons usually live and work in the community; there are films and videotapes; literature exists on most of the topics.

Many congregations have combined youth forums with worship and community building for an integrative Sunday morning at church. These churches serve youth a continental breakfast in a setting which fosters informal conversation. In addition to providing youth an opportunity to talk with friends, the youth ministry leaders of the congregation find this an excellent time for contact with young people. A 45-minute youth forum follows the breakfast. Churches in urban and suburban areas discover this to be one of the few occasions when busy youth from all over the city are able to be together.

Study-action groups

Young people are often passive. Even though they chafe, they go on allowing themselves to be molded and controlled by the mass media, advertisers, employers, parents, school officials, and community leaders. Certainly a large measure of that adult and institutional molding and control is beneficial and in order. Some is not.

Some young people talk a good game but never take the field. They recognize injustice, poverty, and oppression; they criticize those who perpetuate it, yet they never lift a finger to help.

There will be occasions when young peoples' convictions

will press them into action. A current example is concern over nuclear weapons. There will be occasions when youth ministry leaders will need to confront youth with the action inherent in the truth of their convictions. Drugs and teenage pregnancy are such issues.

Education methods

Studies show that young people learn least well when lectured. Education geared to only one or two levels of human consciousness does less well than that beamed to several senses and levels of awareness. Yet the church's primary educational approach is lecture.

Congregations and youth ministry leaders can supplement old educational staples with new approaches. Pastors, youth, and adult leaders can learn to use individualized study, simulation games, mentors, electronic media, case studies, internships, and experiential education in their teaching. Their congregations can help. They can get them trained. Scores of classes, workshops, and seminars are available in these areas. Congregations need to provide the time, money, and equipment needed in order to teach their children well.

Congregational peer culture

Youth ministry can provide young people a place to belong. Peer acceptance and friendship are critical to adolescent development. Most teenagers find these relationships at school and in their neighborhoods. Other youth seem always on the outside. Both these groups of young people need a place where they can relax and find genuine community. It's in these "communities" that young people can best learn respect, forgiveness, and consolation. Here they can experiment with the corporate practice of the presence of God.

Congregational peer cultures can be grounded in the perspectives of faith and the power of the gospel. These perspectives of faith and power issue forth in respectful attitudes about persons and the significance of their relationships. These attitudes foster an atmosphere of openness and honesty. People are free to be themselves. This atmosphere of freedom encourages responsible behavior in which youth respect and care for one another. There is risk. There is affirmation. There are mistakes. People are hurt. There needs to be forgiveness. Within the congregational peer culture, youth can value and live with those different than themselves.

There are a great many vehicles through which congregational peer cultures can be developed. Work projects, camping trips, retreats, and small groups are some of the most common.

They called it *Four S*. Their pastor and one of the congregation's high school seniors started it at Ken's house. All the senior high students in the congregation were invited. Seven came at 7:00 the first Thursday evening. The meeting began with an invitation to join with God and each other in two minutes of silent reflection on the events and rhythms of their day. Then came 15 minutes of group sharing, focused on the question: What's been happening in your life lately? Experiential study of Sunday's gospel lesson came next. The group asked three questions of the text: (1) What does it say? (2) What does it mean? (3) What does it have to do with who I am and what I do?

The meeting ended as the participants sought God's presence through silent or conversational prayer. By 8:00 P.M. the "formal" meeting was finished. Some young people left; others stayed around to talk.

Many youth in that congregation came to call the groups their "church home." It was here they got to know and support each other. They wrestled with personal issues, big and little. Prayer became concrete and life-affirming. Friendships developed that extended beyond the walls of Ken's home and their years in high school. Sunday morning sermons looked different when a text they had studied was preached and more than once the sermons were influenced by the insights shared with the pastor as he met with one of the groups.

Peer counseling

Young people live in a troubled world. Sometimes the struggles are their own; sometimes the troubles belong to their friends; sometimes they belong to their parents. By the time they are 25 years old, adolescents and young adults will have lived through a world marred by chemical abuse, suicide, anorexia, stress, accident, poverty, teenage pregnancy, the threat of nuclear holocaust, and family conflict. A few young people will not survive the journey. Some will barely make it. Others will leave this period deeply scarred.

Adults can be of significant but limited help to young people facing these struggles. Parents, teachers, pastors, and counselors possess the maturity and expertise to provide invaluable assistance, but usually get involved after matters have reached the crisis stage. Often this is too late. These adults have no access whatever to large numbers of youth in trouble. For some adolescents their alienation from adults is at the heart of their struggle. Other adolescents don't trust adults with their problems. Consequently, the earliest and only assistance available to many troubled young people comes from their peers.

The vice-principal called Jennifer's mother. He was upset. Jennifer had been spotted leaving the football game with Sally, a girl obviously high on some drug. He didn't want Jennifer and Sally hanging around with one another and asked Jennifer's mother to assist him in following through on his strategy for separating them. Jennifer's mother did not give him much support. She did find a private moment late that night in which to talk with her daughter about the call and offer her help. At first the conversation was halting and strained; yet, because there was trust and respect which had been developed over the years, Jennifer told her mother of Sally's drug problems and of her efforts to help her friend.

Sally had in fact been stoned at the football game. Jennifer and her friend Betty had taken Sally home, and Betty had stayed with her all night. Sally's dad was a hard-driving authoritarian who expected Sally to be like her sister. Sally's mom was caught between Sally and her father. Sally felt rejected and was confused. She intermittently hated her father and sought his approval. As her alienation from her family had grown, Sally had become dependent on her boyfriend and with him had started taking drugs. Now Sally was addicted and was often stoned.

Sally trusted Jennifer and Betty. Both girls cared about her and had more than once helped her out of a jam. They were trying to get her off the drugs. Now they were stuck. They wanted to help; they didn't want to be narks; they didn't know where to turn. Jennifer's mother didn't know either. Together they searched for some help. They discovered a church in the community which held a peer counseling group where teenagers supported one another and honed their ability to care for others in trouble. Jennifer joined the group. Betty was skeptical. Three months later Jennifer was able to get Sally to see a chemical dependency counselor. Although Sally never reconciled with her parents, through the treatment she managed to stay off drugs and do passing work at school.

Peer counseling groups draw together both troubled and healthy young people for mutual support and caregiving education. The group's supportive atmosphere assists youth with the pressures of caring for another. The abilities developed in the group process are many of the same skills needed in the care of troubled friends. The group becomes a place to work on alternative approaches to specific caregiving situations faced by participants. Within the group, a wide variety of problems facing teenagers can be studied and counseling skills developed. Participants learn how to make good referrals. They develop referral networks. They give attention to the role of faith and the church in healing, guiding, reconciling, and sustaining.

Peer counseling groups need qualified leadership. Youth ministry leaders and pastors with backgrounds in counseling are available in many congregations. If there is no qualified person, someone can be trained. Workshops and training programs are available. Barbara Varenhorst's *Peer Counseling*[3] provides an excellent format for getting started.

Focus on special events

Many exciting youth ministry activities integrate worship, proclamation, education, communion, and service. Four outstanding opportunities available to every congregation are explored more fully here.

Youth gatherings

Youth gatherings are multidimensional experiences which offer young people opportunities rarely available within a single congregation. Youth gatherings, conventions, and congresses now exist at international, ecumenical, denominational, nondenominational, and regional levels. They offer excellence of worship, proclamation, education, communion, and service in a single event. For many young men and women, these events are one of the highlights of their adolescent and young adult faith experience.

Coupled with the event itself, youth leaders can use preparation, travel, life together, and follow-up to build support, intensity, and visibility in congregational youth ministry. Most gatherings, conventions, and congresses have workshops for youth ministry leaders. Youth and adults can use these workshops and the activities of the gathering to stimulate new ideas and develop greater skills for their work in the congregation.

These events usually place young people alongside Christian brothers and sisters from other congregations, communities, denominations, and countries. Sometimes a few youth in a single congregation feel isolated and alone. Parochialism can breed stereotypes and narrow biases. Gathering with hundreds or thousands of other youth breaks open these biases and builds bridges with those who are different.

Youth ministry leaders need to carefully plan the use of such events. They need to ask: How often should our congregation attend such an event? What type of event shall we attend? How will we use getting there, being there, and returning to the greatest advantage for our youth? Will attendance be limited only to the youth who can afford it? Will those youth attending become a clique, separated from the larger youth ministry of the congregation? Will preparation and attendance distort the integrative focus of the congregation's youth ministry? The questions abound. The point is: these events do not carry themselves. They can be a mixed blessing. If carefully used, the gatherings are excellent opportunities for local youth ministry leaders and their colleagues around the world to enrich the faith and life of young people.

Camps, expeditions, and trips offer short periods of intense youth ministry in unique settings. Busy young people have hectic, conflicting schedules. Youth ministry leaders have difficulty finding common times for youth to be together. If scheduled well in advance, adolescents and young adults can arrange their time in order to attend these special events.

The events' intensity encourages young people and their leaders to know each other as well as learn and work together at deeper levels. There is no end to the settings available to become new sanctuaries, classrooms, pulpits, shared experiences, and fields of service.

Camps

Camps of every kind and description have been around a long time. Their unique settings invite creative programming. Usually they offer well-conceived ministry activities carried on by capable staffs which are already in place. Camps can be used as resting places, work sites, sanctuaries, laboratories, and playgrounds. Camp staffs are among the most informed and best trained youth ministers in the church. They can be tapped for leadership training workshops in congregations. They offer potential candidates for those congregations seeking youth ministry staff associates.

Youth ministry leaders have a rich array of well-developed campsites available at almost any level of convenience. These camps come at varying though considerable cost. Youth ministry leaders might well find occasion for choosing less expensive "undeveloped" campsites. Many churches have developed their own "camp staffs" and use country churches, farmsteads, state parks, private lake places, ranches, inner city churches, or mountain hideaways for their camps.

Expeditions

Expeditions provide experiential learning opportunities rarely available anywhere else. They might carry young people into the majesty of the mountains, the solitude of the desert, or the expanse of the ocean. They can plunge youth into the poverty of the ghetto or the wheels of government. Expeditions challenge bodies, minds, and spirits; they carry individuals and groups beyond old boundaries. Young people are forced to look at God's world differently. New and different situations call for attitudes and skills never considered before. Worlds break open. Limits become harsh. Reality stands out in bold relief. Expeditions provide individuals and communities opportunities to shape clear identities and construct expanded world views. Independence and dependence unite in interdependence with nature and other people.

Some churches use expeditions to build community. Others use them for leadership training. Expeditions can build individual character and enhance self-esteem. Expeditions to communities caught in the web of injustice become transformational experiences. Expeditions are extraordinary. They are not for everyone. Youth ministry leaders will need to use them with care and boldness.

Travel trips

Canoe, car, and bike trips can provide youth ministry leaders access to people, places, and processes as well as imagery and experiences that enrich young people's faith. Trips can be used for many of the same purposes as camps and expeditions. There are some distinct advantages to trips, however. There is greater flexibility and economy. They can be leisurely or stressful. They can be done at little or great cost. One can go almost anywhere. They can be a few hours or weeks in length. Small or large groups can go. Some young people have little opportunity to travel; some youth have little opportunity to live and work cooperatively with those their own age. Youth ministry leaders can tailor a trip to meet almost any situation.

Retreats

Retreats have become a staple in youth ministry. Most youth leaders use them. Their popularity is an indication of their effectiveness with young people of all ages. However, retreats can be poorly or even badly used. Some youth ministry leaders expect "going away to an exciting place" to carry a weekend. Most often they come away disappointed, sometimes vowing never to go again.

Retreats need to be well-planned. Important questions need to be asked about a retreat's purpose and program. Congregational youth leaders might want to develop a team of persons with varying responsibilities who can expedite transportation, cooking, worship, community-building, and recreation that can be tailored to the theme and major programming of a particular retreat. They might want to work up some model formats that can be revised and refined with use. A library of sites, models, and resources could be developed. Some congregations have youth ministry retreat traditions that become rites of passage for their young people.

Congregational and peer youth ministry activities are powerful channels for Christ's mission for, by, and with youth. But there can be more. Faith is also a very personal matter, sometimes best known and expressed through one-to-one and individual experience. We turn there next.

12

Individual Youth Ministry Activities

Private worship

Providing youth with a personal approach to God and a disciplined approach to their own development can be one of youth ministry's significant contributions. Several straightforward journaling formats exist. C. S. Lewis and Martin Bell are representative authors of intriguing literature available for their reading. Young people can be taught to devotionally read Scripture and pray.

Adolescents and young adults need meaningful sanctuaries, symbols, and experiences of God. Youth ministries can provide them. Structured solitude among mountain streams, group prayer at ocean sunsets, quiet campfires in darkened forests, and shared conversation on moonlit lakes, draw sanctuaries and symbols from nature. A 10:00 P.M. communion at the church, supportive prayer around a friend's hospital bed, memorial services at the gravesites of their peers, or singing folk songs in Appalachia at the end of the work camp day draw sanctuaries and symbols from history. Adolescents can be encouraged to find their own sanctuaries within the common and the ordinary. They can be assisted in developing art forms pregnant with their own ideas of God. Journals and pastoral conversation deepen their experience and expression of that which is life-giving, holy, and worthy of allegiance. The leadership and resources exist. Those who minister in the church are channels and catalysts for their implementation.

Young people are spirit; they embody thoughts and feelings, morals and values, meanings and beliefs. Every adolescent and young adult has a stance toward life. This stance shapes over a lifetime. It is a spiritual journey. Michael Warren suggests youth ministry is to provide opportunities for young people to attend to this spiritual journey. It means attending to the following questions:

1. What has it been like for you, this journey you've been on?
2. Where do you think you are headed?
3. Who have been the most important who's in your life so far?
4. What aches and pains have you had?
5. What has helped you be most alive on the journey? What have been the spectacular sights that took your breath away?
6. What in your journey so far do you most prize? Of what are you most proud? What would you never want to have done differently?
7. What are your dreams for the future?
8. What matters preoccupy your imagination?
9. What do you want your legacy to the race or to your loved ones to be when you are gone? What do you stand for?
10. What has the religious dimension of your life been so far? What has the Christian dimension been?[1]

Of course not all these questions will be explored explicitly or at once. Many will be probed again and again. Young people need worship which assists them in celebrating these life questions and their answers.

Telling faith's story

Youth ministry can help youth know and tell their faith stories. It can equip gifted youth and adults for bearing witness to the gospel of Jesus Christ. Some youth and adults are particularly gifted in proclaiming the gospel to those who do not believe. An increasing number of young people have rejected the Christian faith or have never heard the gospel. Youth ministry can reach out to these persons who do not know and experience the truth, love, and freedom of God in Jesus Christ.

Every Christian young man and woman has a faith story. Ever since their birth, God has been graciously supplying them life. Since those early beginnings, God has taken up a unique relationship with each young person. That faith story has included a journey with other persons of faith. No two faith stories are the same. Each faith story is vital to the continuing faith stories of others. Young people need the ongoing mutual conversation of God's people. The story of God's life-giving presence in these young men and women will be the genuine proclamation of the gospel many of their friends and colleagues are yearning to hear.

Opening the mutual conversation of faith among God's people and equipping youth and adults to speak of their faith and the gospel is difficult work. Many youth have grown up in families and churches where faith is a private matter better kept to oneself. The image of the Bible-banging buttonholer on the street has left many adolescents and young adults disdainful of Christians who try to force their faith on others. Some youth know so little of their faith tradition or their own faith that they are embarrassed to identify themselves as believers, even in casual conversation.

There are a number of effective formats for this difficult process. One of the finest is outlined in Edward Markquart's *Witnesses for Christ.*[2] Another simple process uses an individual's faith autobiography as the vehicle for identifying and expressing one's beliefs. These faith autobiographies are sketched in diaries over time, using a few basic questions to trigger the individual's thinking. Youth and adults are to ask: Where do I find life? What is most important to me? How do I cope? Where do I belong? How do I express my love? What are my sources of hope? What do all these say about my faith? Where have I seen God at work in my life? What are my images of God? A small group is created to provide an intentional and supportive atmosphere. One-to-one conversations become exercises in careful listening and speaking about each other's faith stories. Everyday discourse becomes the occasion for weaving faith-talk into one's common parlance. These small groups started among youth ministry leaders can become training ground for youth and adults who can lead subsequent groups of youth in doing the same.

This process can be developed slowly and deliberately. It can create numerous cadres of youth who support one another's faith and life through mutual conversation and consolation. It fosters confidence in individual youth for telling their faith story among their friends and inviting them to church.

Visitation

Visitation is the heart of youth ministry. Faith is relational. Relationships are particularly crucial in the faith of adolescents. Every young person in a congregation can have at least one adult who establishes a significant relationship with them. Pastors, youth ministry staff associates, teachers, youth choir directors, and youth sponsors can be visitors. Other adults can be recruited if necessary. Each of these adults needs to be trained in the art of caring conversation. One person on the youth committee should coordinate and oversee their work.

The aims of the youth ministry visitation process are straightforward and basic:
1. Establish and maintain contact with the young person on behalf of the congregation.
2. Get to know, understand, and encourage the person in her faith and life.

3. Regularly remember the teenager in prayer.
4. Encourage the young person in her participation in worship.
5. Provide mutual conversation and caring.

In many cases these relationships will deepen and develop with visitors becoming faith mentors and confidants. A list of youth counseling resources needs to be available should the visitors need it. Delicate information must be kept in the strictest confidence.

The key characteristics of a youth visitor are known. Youth visitors are persons of: (1) honest faith, (2) integrity, (3) interest in people, (4) warmth, and (5) empathy. These capacities exist in a wide variety of people of differing ages in every congregation. Visitation can be taught to those who have the interest and aptitude. Persons engaged in visiting youth can be supported in their ministry. There is not much time and there are not many places in which to visit young people, but if the task is creatively and strategically approached, it can be accomplished.

What is visitation? It is the art of caring presence and mutual conversation. Sometimes it demonstrates sensitivity and affirmation through showing up at an important event or sending a card or letter honoring a significant day or accomplishment. More often it takes the form of significant engagement with a young person in conversation.

Mutual, caring conversation is multidimensional. For each person in the conversation it is: (1) description—giving language to one's world, (2) reaction—getting at the emotional responses in one's experience, (3) reflection—exploring the meanings and beliefs of one's life, and (4) action—choosing to act in love upon the truth discovered in oneself and the other.

People can learn to initiate and engender such conversation with young people. In doing so, they care for that young person and foster that young person's caring for herself and others. In this process there is knowing and being known. Personal language is given to the truth, beauty, and good as well as the evil in one's own life. Participants love and are loved. People care and are cared for. The truth and love of faith in Jesus Christ can be experienced and made known. Acceptance, confrontation, forgiveness, and restoration can be personally mediated. The gospel can do its work.

Each congregation and youth visitor will find times and places for visitation of youth. A few times and places have great potential and are named here. There are times of beginning, such as a pastor visiting a young person who was recently baptized or a confirmand the summer before he starts confirmation, visiting each young person at the beginning of junior high school or when she has been chosen for an athletic team; there are times of ending, such as finishing confirmation, graduating from high school, the death of a grandparent, or the breakup of a special relationship; there are times of celebration, such as getting a driver's license, getting an award, turning 13 or 18 or 21; there are times of getting away, such as youth conventions, travel trips, work camps, or Bible camps. There are places of personal identification, such as a young person's home, classes at school, athletic field/court, place of work, recreational place, or car; places of eating, such as breakfast at a restaurant, lunch at the school cafeteria, a picnic in the park, or pizza after studying; places of significant events, such as the cemetery, an accident scene, concert hall, or the church sanctuary or altar. Every congregation could greatly enhance its youth ministry by providing substantial expense monies for food and travel for its pastor and the others called to do this visitation ministry with youth.

What does one do in youth ministry? One involves youth in the life and mission of the whole congregation so that the congregation becomes youth-friendly and taps the strength of its young people. One develops a lively peer ministry where young people can be together, identify with Christ, and grow through struggling with the issues of their faith and its expression. One focuses on each young person, and attends to their unique faith and life pilgrimage. Thorough, effective youth ministry is multi-leveled and wholistic.

This book ends where it began. Five critical youth ministry questions have been explored. Five responses to those critical questions have been articulated. Those responses emerge from one man's love of Christ and teenagers. Thanks for joining in the exploration. Now the questions and responses are the reader's. God's grace and peace as in your love of Christ and teenagers you forge your own ministry with youth.

Appendix 1

Annotated List of Youth Ministry Resources

Witness resources

Clown Ministry, Floyd Schaffer and Penne Sewall, (Atlanta: Group Books, 1984).

Describes how to begin a clown ministry. Includes 30 detailed skits and over 50 short clowning ideas.

Evangelizing Youth, What Christians Can Learn From One Another, Glen C. Smith, Editor, (Wheaton: Tyndale, 1985).

Everyone from the Assemblies of God, to Youth for Christ, to Gary Downing, to Pope John II gives his/her ideas and insights into the evangelizing of youth.

Quest for Better Preaching, Edward Markquart, (Minneapolis: Augsburg, 1985).

While not written primarily about preaching to youth, this book sets forth the principles of effective preaching to young people. The chapter on the use of "SIA's" is particularly fine in this regard.

Witnesses for Christ, Edward Markquart, (Minneapolis: Augsburg, 1983).

Although written for adults, this course can be easily adapted for instructing youth in telling their faith story to each other and their friends.

Community-building resources

Building Community in Youth Groups, Denny Rydberg, (Loveland, Colo.: Group Books, 1985).

A good place to start for a resource on group building. This book has many different approaches to boundary breaking, affirming, and helping young people to open up and share with each other.

Great Ideas for Small Youth Groups, Wayne Rice, (Zondervan/ Youth Specialties, 1985).

Eighty percent of church youth groups are small. Rice discusses the advantages and disadvantages of the small youth group, highlights the strengths of "smallness," and offers several hundred program ideas for the small group.

The Group Retreat Book, Arlo Reichter, Editor, (Loveland, Colo.: Group Books, 1983).

A complete retreat planning guide, giving hints for every aspect of the "nuts and bolts" of putting together a retreat from publicity and transportation to recipes and resources. Then come 34 "ready-to-use" ("ready-to-alter") different types of junior high/high school retreat programs.

The Youth Group Meeting Guide, Richard W. Bimler, Editor, (Loveland, Colo.: Group Books, 1984).

Eighty-eight "ready-to-use" meeting outlines arranged alphabetically by subject . . . anxiety to vocation. The book also has quite a large section on the "how-to" of meetings. A great resource for those just starting out and those trying to get out of a rut.

Creative Communication and Community Building, Edited by Wayne Rice, John Roberto, and Mike Yaconelli (Winona, Minn.: St. Mary's Press, Christian Brothers Publications, 1981).

One hundred and fourteen great community-building ideas. Group building, helping individuals to share themselves in a group, and a short introduction to group dynamics, and of course . . . ideas.

The New Games Book and *More New Games Book,* Andrew Flugelman, Editor, (New York: Dolphin/Doubleday, 1976).

Games for two to two hundred built on the "play hard, play fair, nobody hurt" philosophy. Often there is no winner, stressing cooperation rather than competition.

Teaching resources

To Set One's Heart: Belief and Teaching in the Church, Sara Little, (Atlanta: John Knox Press, 1983).

Uses belief formation as an organizing center for the church's teaching ministry. Offers five models of teaching and shows how each contributes to faith development.

The Giving Book, Creative Resources for Senior High Ministry, Paul M. Thompson and Joani Schultz, (Atlanta: John Knox Press, 1985).

A blend of recreational and serious study. In-depth exploration of life, faith, scriptural truths, and treasures based on the concept of "giving." Contains a leader's guide.

Creative Bible Studies, Dennis Benson, (Loveland, Colo.: Group Books, 1985).

Designed to explore Matthew, Mark, Luke, John, and Acts, this book provides 401 Bible study ideas presented as activity/study models. They are arranged in the order the passages appear in the Bible.

The Teenage Body Book, Kathy McCoy and Charles Wibbelsman, M.D., (New York: Simon and Schuster, revised and updated 1984).

Honest, no-nonsense answers to the hundreds of questions young people have about these vital years in their lives. Covers every aspect of what it means to be physical, sexual, and emotional during adolescent years in a frank and informative way.

Adolescent Spirituality, Pastoral Ministry for High School and College Youth, Charles M. Shelton, S.J., (Chicago: Loyola University Press, 1983).

Father Shelton integrates counseling and developmental psychology, pastoral theology and spirituality, and offers a complete overview of adolescent growth covering a wide range of topics including moral, spiritual, vocational, interpersonal, and cognitive development. A great book for the person in youth work who has anything to do with education of young people! It lays out summaries of Piaget, Erikson, Fowler, Perry, and others in the adolescent development field, while at the same time exploring issues and offering advice to the educator.

Service resources

Hunger: Understanding the Crisis through Games, Dramas, and Songs, Patricia Houck Sprinkle, (Atlanta: John Knox Press, 1980).

Compendium of activities for exploring world hunger. Classifies activities by age group, size of group, time needed, etc.

Ideas for Social Action, Anthony Campolo, (El Cajon, Calif.: Youth Specialties, 1983).

A handbook on mission and service for Christian young people. Common sense advice and solid rationale for such service from one who has done a lot of social action work with/through groups of young people. Dr. Campolo is professor of sociology at Eastern College in St. Davids, PA. The book highlights a wide range of service projects and has contributions by several authors.

A Chance to Serve, Peer Minister's Handbook and *A Chance to Serve, A Leader's Manual for Peer Ministry,* Brian Reynolds, (Winona, Minn.: St. Mary's Press, Christian Brothers Publications, 1984).

This is not just another leadership retreat; rather it is a formal, systematic program that offers the average teenage young person opportunities for growth in faith, for community building, and for leadership training. Designed to help you make the move from theory to action in terms of peer ministry.

The Compassion Project, Compassion International, 3955 Cragwood Drive, P.O. Box 7000, Colorado Springs, CO 80933, 1-800-336-7676.

A resource "package" of materials designed to help young people discover the truth about world poverty and how they can make a difference. Cassette tapes, slides, two movies (or videos), a leader's guide, etc. This is free to use, though you will be encouraged to consider Compassion's child sponsorship.

Let it Growl . . . for thirty hours and help hungry people. World Vision International, c/o Planned Famine, Box O, Pasadena, CA 91109.

Materials for a structured retreat on world hunger. They will send the materials at no cost but highly suggest that your group also use the retreat as a fund raiser for World Vision.

General resources

1985 Resource Directory for Youth Workers, Francine Phillips, Editor, (Nashville: Abingdon Press or El Cajon, CA: Youth Specialties, 1985).

Addresses for resources of every kind on every subject listed by category. Send for catalogs to:

Abingdon Press
201 Eighth Avenue South
Nashville, TN 37202

Argus Communications
P.O. Box 5000
Allen, TX 75002

Augsburg Publishing House
426 South Fifth Street
Box 1209
Minneapolis, MN 55440

Concordia Publishing House
3558 South Jefferson Avenue
St. Louis, MO 63118

Educational Products Division
Word, Inc.
7300 Imperial
Waco, TX 76796

Group Books
P.O. Box 481
Loveland, CO 80539

Group Magazine
P.O. Box 481
Loveland, CO 80539

John Knox Press
341 Ponce de Leon Avenue N.E.
Atlanta, GA 30308

Judson Press
Box 851
Valley Forge, PA 19482

National Teacher Education Project
7214 East Granada Road
Scottsdale, AZ 85257

Paulist Press
997 Macarthur Blvd.
Mahwah, NJ 07430

Harper and Row San Francisco
Winston-Seabury Press
Icehouse One
Suite 401

151 Union Street
San Francisco, CA 94111

Youth Specialties
1224 Greenfield Drive
El Cajon, CA 92021

Youthworker
1224 Greenfield Drive
El Cajon, CA 92021

Appendix 2

A Congregational and Community Youth Ministry Survey

Purpose: Identify the past and present state of youth ministry in a congregation and community.

I.   Congregational youth ministry history

Focus on the last five to 10 years. Speak with six to nine key people:

A. A former pastor.

B. Two high school students active in the church.

C. Two young adults who grew up in the church.

D. Two parents of young adults.

E. A past president of the congregation.

F. A youth and young adult leader from the past.

G. Two confirmands.*

H. Follow the suggestions of these people as to who might know more.

---

*This is an example of a survey I use with churches which have a confirmation tradition. Other traditions can modify the survey for their own use.

These questions might be asked:

1. Where have youth been present in the life of the congregation?
2. What has been the congregation's attitude about youth?
3. How have young people and their parents viewed the confirmation ministry?
4. Have young people respected and valued the pastor?
5. Have young people felt welcome here?
6. Has there been a youth program? A youth group? Who's been involved? What's it been like?
7. What contribution has this congregation made in the lives of young people?
8. Who has been responsible for youth ministry?

II.   Community youth ministry history

Focus on the last five to 10 years. Speak to a representative person from each congregation, parachurch group, and ecumenical agency in the community. The group listed above might also be asked these questions:

1. Where have youth (particularly Christian youth) been present in the life of the community?
2. How are youth perceived in the community?
3. What is your congregation, group, or agency doing in ministry with youth?
4. What contributions are youth (particularly Christian youth) making in the community?
5. What needs of youth are being/not being met in the community?
6. What are the community's institutions' (schools, law enforcement, business, social service, etc.) attitudes about the churches', parachurch groups', and ecumenical agencies' work with youth?

III. **Congregational and community youth summary, analysis, and implications**
   A. Develop a summary of the findings.
   B. Analysis: Look at strengths, weaknesses, assumptions, possible resources, and coalitions as well as challenges.
   C. Draw implications for the future.

The findings of this survey will guide the congregation's youth ministry representative and pastor in taking the next steps in their development of the congregation's ministry with youth.

Appendix 3

A Community Field Study of Youth

A field study is a careful gathering and analysis of information about a designated geographic and cultural area. Pertinent sources of information are tapped in order to accurately describe the community: (1) geographically, (2) economically, (3) vocationally, (4) educationally, (5) racially, (6) religiously, (7) sociologically, (8) politically, (9) "communicationally," and (10) recreationally. Attention is given to the effect of these on young people. Care is taken to understand how youth are seen through the eyes of: (1) representative youth, (2) parents, (3) school officials, (4) law enforcement agents, (5) youth employers, (6) youth organization leaders, (7) political officials, (8) youth-oriented business people, and (9) church leaders. Analysis seeks to identify youth: (1) subcultures, (2) leadership, (3) beliefs, (4) values, (5) capabilities, (6) concerns, (7) needs, (8) problems, and (9) contributions. Implications are drawn for ministry. Field studies are provocative, especially if youth and adults gather and analyze data, and implement subsequent strategies together.

Appendix 4

A Conversational Community Youth Inquiry

Purpose: Identify the gifts and needs of the young people of a church and community.

I. **Inquiry leaders**

   The congregation's youth ministry representative and the pastor will lead the inquiry. These two persons need to select and personally invite the participants. The YMR should lead the inquiry process.

II. **Inquiry participants**

   Eighteen to thirty persons will be invited to participate. Young people in the congregation need to be consulted as to who can best represent each of the following groups from among the youth:

   A. Two seventh graders.
   B. Two eighth graders.
   C. Two ninth graders.
   D. Two tenth graders.
   E. Two eleventh graders.
   F. Two twelfth graders.
   G. Two young adults.

From among the adults:

A. The president of the congregation.
B. Two junior high parents.
C. Two senior high parents.
D. A junior high Sunday school teacher.
E. A senior high Sunday school teacher.
F. An adult youth ministry leader.
G. A "favorite" junior high school teacher.
H. A "favorite" senior high school teacher.
I. A probation officer.
J. A community youth employer.

Representative diversity in sexual, racial, and socioeconomic backgrounds needs to be kept in mind.

III. Inquiry process

The participants will be personally invited to a single three-hour workshop. Early Sunday evening is often a good time. There will be two tasks for the group: (1) identify the gifts and needs of the youth in the community and (2) draw implications from these for the congregation's ministry. A medium-sized room with movable chairs is desirable. Paper, pencils, newsprint, a marker, and masking tape will be needed.

After introductions have been quickly made, the group is divided into groups of four or five persons. Each group should include at least two youth. The groups will be formed around key dimensions of young people's lives. Four or five persons should be asked to consider the community youths' gifts and needs in each of the following areas:

A. Inner life (thoughts, feelings, dreams, etc.).
B. Relationships and groups.
C. Economics.
D. Heroes and symbols.
E. Values and life-styles.
F. Beliefs and attitudes about church.

Each group needs to appoint a recorder. Each group will have 30 minutes to identify and discuss gifts and needs in their particular area. Then 30 minutes of reporting and plenary discussion will ensue with the YMR leading the group and the pastor recording the information on the newsprint. After a 20-minute refreshment break the groups are invited to reconvene and spend 30 minutes exploring the implications of their information for the life and mission of the church. Again, each group will be asked to report its finding with ample time provided for discussion.

Before the meeting is adjourned, each person is thanked and invited to sign on if they should like to participate in the congregation's youth ministry development process.

IV. Inquiry summary, analysis, and follow-up

The YMR and the pastor need to discuss and analyze the workshop's findings and prepare them for distribution to the participants, church council, and congregational youth ministry leadership.

The results of this inquiry will give the youth leaders of the congregation a solid sense of the potential role the congregation might play in channeling their young people's gifts and responding to their needs.

Over against the backdrop of the history of the congregation's and community's youth ministry and informed by their awareness of the gifts and needs of the youth in the congregation and community, a congregation's leaders need to develop a vision to guide them in developing ministry with young people. The gospel message and its implications for the church's life and mission can supply this guiding vision.

Appendix 5

A Theological Exploration of the Gospel's Message and the Church's Mission

Purpose: Identify the congregational youth leadership's understanding of the gospel with its implications for the church's mission and ministry with youth.

I. Leadership

The pastor and the congregation's youth ministry representative should co-lead this exploration. The YMR should guide the process; the pastor should present a brief (two-three page) statement of the gospel message and its implications for the church's mission and ministry with youth. (He might use the one provided in Chapter 3 of this book.) The YMR and pastor should share the responsibility of personally inviting the participants.

II. Participants

Ten to 15 persons should be invited to participate. Young people in the congregation should be consulted as to who best represents each of the following categories of people. From among the youth:

A. Two junior high persons.
B. Two senior high persons.
C. Two young adults.
D. Two young people who have youth ministry leadership roles in the congregation.

Young people should be chosen who can readily express their faith. From among the adults:

A. Two junior high parents.
B. Two senior high parents.
C. The president of the congregation.
D. A junior high Sunday school teacher.
E. A senior high Sunday school teacher.
F. Another key adult youth ministry leader in the congregation.
G. If there is an existing youth committee, every member should be invited.

Representative diversity in theological, sexual, racial, and socio-economic backgrounds needs to be kept in mind.

III. Process

The participants need to be personally invited to a single three-hour workshop. Early Sunday evening is often a good time. There will be two tasks for the group: (1) identify their understandings of the gospel message and (2) draw implications from that message for the church's mission and ministry with youth. A medium-sized room with movable chairs is desirable. Paper, pencils, Bibles, newsprint, a marker, and masking tape will be needed.

After brief introductions are made, the pastor will ask each person to write brief sentences summarizing their faith. The group is given eight to 10 minutes to think and write.

Next the pastor makes a 15-minute presentation on the gospel message and its implications for the church's mission with youth. The pastor and the YMR have discussed and agreed upon this statement before the meeting.

After the pastor's presentation the small groups of five to six youth and adults spend 10 minutes sharing and discussing their statements and the pastor's presentation, and 20 minutes drawing implications from their statements and the pastor's for the church's mission and ministry with youth. Next, 15 minutes of group reporting and general discussion ensues.

The evening closes with thanks to the participants and an invitation to join the ministry leadership of the congregation as they continue developing ministry with young people.

IV. Summary, formulation, and follow-up
The YMR and the pastor should discuss and analyze the workshop data. The pastor needs to formulate a youth ministry mission statement in the light of the information gleaned in the workshop. The mission statement should be no longer than two pages. After the YMR and pastor have agreed on the statement, it should be distributed to the workshop participants, presented to the youth committee for further discussion and reformulation, and finally presented to the church council for approval. A sample youth ministry mission statement is provided in Chapter 9 on pages 87-88.

Appendix 6

Developing Youth Ministry Organizational Structure and Process

Purpose: Assess the existing congregational youth ministry structures and processes; organizationally develop structures and processes needed to execute faithful and effective youth ministry throughout the congregation and community.

I. Leadership

The YMR and pastor need to enlist the assistance of the president of the congregation in this effort. If none of these three persons are knowledgeable in organizational development, someone with such knowledge and skill needs to be secured from the congregation or community.

II. Criteria

The YMR, the pastor, and the congregational president need to discuss and agree on the criteria by which they will evaluate the present congregational youth ministry structures and processes. The following are suggested for their consideration:

A. Is there a clearly identified, congregationally elected adult person empowered to oversee and be held accountable for guiding youth ministry in the congregation? Is there an up-to-date job description for this position?

B. Do those responsible for youth ministry have representation on the central decision-making body in the congregation? Usually this will translate into the question: Is there a youth ministry representative on the church council? Normally, this person and the individual above should be the same person.

C. Is there a small group of persons (three to seven) charged with the responsibilities of: (1) formulating policy in youth ministry for the church council to consider, (2) providing advocacy for youth throughout the congregation, (3) providing a forum where youth and adults can regularly discuss congregational life and mission in a trusting atmosphere, (4) considering the gifts and needs of youth in the congregation and community and designing "ministry responses," and (5) developing leadership for youth ministry? These persons need to serve two- to three-year staggered terms. This group's chairperson should sit on the church council and be the congregational youth ministry representative. This group's vice chairperson should be in line to be the next YMR. At least one-half of this group must be youth.

D. Is there a regular pattern of listening to the congregation's youth, setting goals for youth ministry, evaluating the congregation's "youth friendliness," youth ministry programming, and reconsidering the congregation's relationships with the ecumenical youth ministry community?

E. Is there a viable support system for youth and adults doing youth ministry throughout the congregation?

    F. Are youth directly and adequately represented in the congregation's budget?

III. Assessment and reconstruction

The YMR, pastor, and congregational president should prepare an evaluation summary. They need to decide what, if any, changes are needed and strategize as to how, when, and through whom these changes will be made. Support for each other is crucial in this effort. It is important to take all the necessary steps to appropriately involve the congregation in the organization.

IV. Documentation and reassessment

The YMR should see that all new structures are clearly described so that those working within them can understand their roles. The YMR, pastor, and congregational president need to reassess the structures and processes after they have been in place for a year.

Notes

Chapter 2

1. D. S. Amalorpauadass, "Theory of Evangelization," in *Service and Salvation,* Joseph Pathrapankel, ed. (Bangalore, India: Theological Publications, 1973), pp. 37-38.
2. See Appendix 1 for an annotated list of youth ministry witness resources.
3. Ruberick S. French, "Theological Reflections on the Church's Ministry to Youth," in *The New Creation and the New Generation,* Albert H. van den Heuvel, ed. (New York: Friendship Press, 1965), p. 13.
4. See Appendix 1 for an annotated list of youth ministry teaching resources.
5. See Appendix 1 for an annotated list of youth ministry community-building resources.
6. See Appendix 1 for an annotated list of youth ministry service resources.

Chapter 3

1. See Jean Piaget, "Intellectual Evolution from Adolescence to Adulthood," *Human Development* 15 (1972): 1-12.

Chapter 4

1. See Erik H. Erikson, *Identity, Youth and Crisis* (New York: W. W. Norton, 1968).
2. Carol Gilligan, *In a Different Voice* (New York: Harper & Row, 1983).
3. Erikson, pp. 91-141.

4. Gilligan, p. 12.
5. David Myer, *The Inflated Self* (New York: Seabury, 1980), pp. 23-24.
6. Erikson, p. 133.
7. Myer, p. xv.

Chapter 5

1. James Fowler, Stages of Faith (New York; Harper & Row, 1981).
2. Ibid., p. 17.
3. Ibid., p. 274.
4. The Princeton Religious Research Study, Princeton, N. J., *Religion in America, 1979–80*, section on "Focus on Youth and Family."
5. Search Institute, *Study of Early Adolescence*, p. 14.
6. See Lawrence Kohlberg, "The Development of Children's Orientation Toward a Moral Order," *Vita Humina* 6 (1963): 11-33.
7. Ronald Goldman, *Readiness for Religion* (New York: Seabury, 1970), p. 204.
8. Merton Strommen, *Five Cries of Youth* (New York: Harper & Row, 1973).
9. Goldman, p. 174.

Chapter 6

1. The themes articulated here are based on data drawn from the University of Michigan's Institute for Social Research's ongoing study entitled: "Monitoring the Future," by Gerald Bachman and Lloyd Johnston.
2. See Search Institute's survey (call 612/870-9511 for more information), "Becoming the Gift," and the field survey in Appendix 3.

Chapter 9

1. See Appendix 2: A Congregational and Community Youth Ministry Survey.
2. See Appendix 3: A Community Field Study of Youth.
3. See Appendix 4: A Conversational Community Youth Inquiry.
4. See Appendix 5: A Theological Exploration of the Gospel's Message and the Church's Mission.
5. See Appendix 6: Developing Youth Ministry Organizational Structure and Process.

Chapter 10

1. C. S. Lewis, *The Chronicles of Narnia* (New York: MacMillan, 1950).
2. John Westerhoff III, *Bringing Up Your Children in the Christian Faith* (Minneapolis: Winston, 1980).

3. Arch Books (St. Louis: Concordia).
4. Walter Wangerin Jr., *The Bible: Its Story for Children* (New York: Rand McNally, 1981).
5. Martin Bell, *The Way of the Wolf* (New York: Seabury, 1979).
6. Martin Bell, *The Return of the Wolf* (New York: Seabury, 1985).
7. Lewis, *The Chonicles of Narnia* (see above).
8. Hannah Hurnard, *Hind's Feet on High Places* (Wheaton: Tyndale, 1977).
9. See Roland Martinson, *Ministry with Families* (Minneapolis: Augsburg, 1986), Chap. 4.
10. See Don Dinkmeyer and Gary D. McKay, *STEP: Systematic Training for Effective Parenting* (Circle Pines, Minn.: American Guidance Service).
11. Merton and Irene Strommen, *Five Cries of Parents* (New York: Harper & Row, 1985).
12. Lois and Joel Davitz, *How to Live Almost Happily with Your Teenager* (Minneapolis: Winston, 1982).
13. Anita Farel, ed., *For Parents of Early Adolescents* (Chapel Hill, N.C.: Center for Early Adolescence, 1982.
14. The Strong-Campbell Vocational Test is available from guidance counselors at local high schools.

Chapter 11

1. Lyman Coleman, *Celebration, Discovery,* and other Serendipity books (Nashville: Abingdon).
2. Dennis Benson, *401 Creative Ways to Study the Bible* (Loveland, Colo.: Group, 1985).
3. Barbara Varenhorst, *Peer Counseling.* Available from Barbara Varenhorst, 350 Grove Dr., Portola Valley CA 94025.

Chapter 12

1. Michael Warren, *Youth and the Future of the Church* (New York: Seabury, 1982), pp. 62-63.
2. Edward Markquart, *Witnesses for Christ* (Minneapolis: Augsburg, 1983).